Taquetta flows through the wells of warfare and worship and mantles an apostolic mandate of judging and establishing God's kingdom in people, ministries, communities, and regions. Taquetta travels in foreign missions and throughout the United States. She has mentored and established dance, altar workers, deliverance, and prophetic ministries. Taquetta ministers in the areas of fine arts, all manners of prayer, fivefold ministry, deliverance, healing, miracles, atmospheric worship, and empowers and train people in their destiny and life's vision.

Connect with Taquetta and KSM at kingdomshifters.com or via Facebook. For more information regarding Bishop Jackie Green at Jgmenternational.org.

Foreword

This book is for anyone who would like to gain greater knowledge and understanding of fivefold ministry through dance. Detailed revelation and insight is provided to enlighten the reader about the function of each specific fivefold office through the realm of dance. Apostles, Prophets, Preachers, Teachers, and Evangelists all work together for the equipping of the saints and the advancing of God's kingdom in the earth. As ministers of dance advancing the kingdom through movement, it is important to have the fundamental teachings and implementation of fivefold ministry within our personal dance ministry, as well as our teams. Fivefold ministry and dance exemplifies the need for team ministry and the importance of the function of each office. The fivefold ministry endows us with distinct administrative power and authority to carry out the plans and will of God for the people and regions we minister to. This increases our ability to effectively establish what God is speaking and doing as we minister because we equip, empower, and build through our movement. The reader will be able to see themselves within the writings of this book as the author intricately breaks down the various identifying factors of the fivefold offices. Some readers will identify most with one office or multiple functions within more than one office. As your identity is enlightened, the execution of God's unique anointing and grace on your life will grow more keen, clear, and strong. Greater understanding will fill you about your godly design, who you are, and why. Foundations of your identity will receive cultivation as you receive the impartation of this

Book Synopsis

***"Dance and the Fivefold Ministry,"** explores the importance of dancers shifting from operating in gifts and talents to walking in the calling and destiny of that God has designed for their lives. The word states in Ephesians 4:11-12, that apostles, prophets, evangelists, pastors, and teachers where given to the body of Christ to assist with equipping and perfecting it, and for the further advancement of God's kingdom. As dancers we are not only the voice and heart of the Lord, but His very movement, and therefore, are vital conduits to establishing and activating his kingdom in the earth realm.*

For too long many dancers have allowed being ostracized, criticized, religion, tradition, and peculiarity, hinder them from receiving and accepting who God has called them to be, and thus, it has caused some misalignment where the full governmental rule and reign of God's calling on our lives are off centered. As we enter this era of significant governmental rule, it is very important that we shift from just being performers, entertainers, program fillers, etc., to effective ministers of dance that operate in the mantle that Jesus left the church. This is important for seeing His work being done in and through us, and so that the fullness of our calling and destiny come to pass. This book provides revelation, knowledge, deliverance, and healing as one comes into a greater understanding of the call of dance and how it relates to fivefold ministry.

Dance and the Fivefold Ministry

TaquettaBaker@Kingdomshifters.com

(Website) Kingdomshifters.com
Connect with Taquetta via Facebook or Youtube

Taquetta's Bio

Taquetta Baker is the founder of Kingdom Shifters Ministries (KSM). She has authored fourteen books and two decree CD's. Taquetta has a Master's Degree in Community Counseling with an emphasis on Marriage, Children and Family Counseling, a Bachelor's Degree in Psychology and Associates Degree in Business Administration. In addition, Taquetta has a Therapon Belief Therapist Certification from Therapon Institute and has 22 years of professional and Christian Counseling experience.

Taquetta is also gifted at empowering and assisting people with launching ministries, businesses and books and provides mentoring, counseling and vision casting through Kingdom Shifters Kingdom Wellness Program. Taquetta serves on the Board of Directors for New Day Community Ministries, Inc. of Muncie, IN.

In October 2008, Taquetta graduated from the Eagles Dance Institute under Dr. Pamela Hardy and received her license in the area of liturgical dance. Before launching into her own ministry, Taquetta served at her previous church for 12 years. She was a prophet, pioneer and leader of Shekinah Expressions Dance Ministry, teacher, member of the presbytery board, and overseer of the Altar Workers Ministry. Taquetta receives mentoring and ministry covering from Bishop Jackie Green, Founder of JGM-Enternational PrayerLife Institute (Redlands, AZ), and was ordained as an Apostle on June 7, 2014.

book. No longer will you be just a dancer and a lover of movement, you will know who you are as a minister and carrier of the gospel of Jesus Christ. You will be shifted from flowing in your gift and talent of dance to embodying and resting in your God ordained purpose and calling.

Nina Cook
Founder of Manifold Grace Production Company
Muncie, Indiana

Foreword

It is a magnificent privilege to share a word about Taquetta prior to your journey into Fivefold Ministry and Dance. This book shines a radiant light of revelation on dance ministry in the 21st century church. Taquetta is an honorable woman who operates in Ecclesiastes 9:10, "Whatsoever thy hand findeth to do, do [it] with thy might . . . ." In her vision of dance, she incorporates dramatization, poetry, flags, and a diversity of musical presentation. Each song is developed through scriptural study, prayer, fasting, and worship. The results are always impeccable excellence. Taquetta's assignment includes apostolically planting dance ministries and covering them through teaching and mentoring.

Taquetta's ministry has broken down the spirit of gospel entertainment, released healing and deliverance of sickness, addictions, personal issues, and imparted prophetic words to whole congregations. On a mission trip to the mountains and fishing villages of Jamaica, children were flocking to Taquetta wanting to dance with her as she praised the Lord. Her anointing is as compelling as her smile and is as stunning as her garments. My own spiritual mother used to say, "Holy women are gracious women." Taquetta epitomizes that proverbial insight. Young and old alike are blessed through her ministry. I am in awe of how powerfully God uses Taquetta and of how fearlessly and wholeheartedly she surrenders herself to the move of His presence. Whether she is ministering at a birthday party, family reunion, community event, or at a church service, her ministry literally pours forth and saturates the atmosphere. The Sovereign God has placed a mark of distinction on her dance.

In the strength of heritage, Taquetta is constantly pushing those who minister with her to find higher places of revelation.

She has made sure that all who stand with her consistently elevate in their personal lives and in ministry. As surely as dance celebrates and expresses the Word of the Lord, this unique and exquisite insight into dance and fivefold ministry will bless you over and over again. Taquetta Baker is a powerful young woman who has come to enrich the body of Christ and the world for such a time as this.

Kathy Williams
Founder of New Day Ministries
Muncie, Indiana

Table of Contents

Dance and the Fivefold Ministry

As dancers, it is essential that we break the stronghold of performance over our ministries, and in the kingdom as a whole. We must possess a mindset that dance is ministry, a vital release for the 21st century church, and is essential to shifting atmospheres and establishing the kingdom of God in the earth realm. If we are going to effectively change the face of dance where it is seen as productive ministry that produce kingdom results, we cannot go forth as performers and entertainers, nor can we allow people to treat us as such. We can no longer minister for the sake of showcasing talents, being seen, or letting others use our gift for religious amusement. We can no longer go to churches without fasting and praying first and seeking God for His purpose. We must understand that we are ministers first and that dance is simply how God uses us to speak His word and heart to His people, while establishing His kingdom in the earth.

> **The word says in Proverbs 18:16:**
> *A man's gift maketh room for him, and bringeth him before great men.*

We have made this scripture into a high place within the body of Christ. It is often used to keep people hindered from operating in the things of God. Some feel condemned about going forth when they know what God has spoken. Others are stifled and even spiritually murdered, because instead of being mentored in the things of the Lord, they are shuffled into a corner and demanded to wait until they have proven to those around them that they are worthy of the call upon their lives. And when many finally go forth, they become so comfortable with the rewards and room their gifts make, that some fail to move into the true calling and destiny of God upon their lives.

It is so essential that we break this stronghold off our lives. Especially as dancers who have had to war to breakthrough religious and traditional strongholds that defy the call of dance upon our lives. We must know without a fleeting doubt that our ministry of dance is more than filling a slot in a program or being just another pretty, graceful or fun thing to do at church. We must grasp that dance does effective work in the spirit and natural realm that produces the physical creativity and manifestation of the Lord, and if we continue to remain ignorant of those dynamics, we will never walk in the fullness of our calling as a minister of movement. Consequently, we will not manifest the ministerial fruit that God is calling us to show. We will only ever receive hand claps and people telling us how beautiful our dance is and how they were just so blessed. People will never be saved or transformed. Demons will never be cast out. Strongholds will never be cast down. Principalities of religion, traditionalism, control, and charismatic manipulation will continue to dominate the move of God in people's lives, churches, communities, and nations. The fullness of praise and worship will never break forth with freedom and kingdom liberty will produce kingdom fruit until we grasp the vision that dance is not about who is more talented, our perfected moves, or how we can be as close to the world in using our gifts but still remain saved; people will only see our dance as a talent. The real reason God manifested the art of dance and performing art gifts will continue to be perverted and counterfeited by the enemy, and used as performance and entertainment with minimal fruit of its true purpose. We have been seen as gifted, but our calling will continue to be stifled and taken for granted. One essential truth is that God is progressive, and it takes movement to advance His kingdom in our midst.

The main differences between a dancer and one who ministers the preached word is that one who ministers through words receives more time to get his/her point across, is viewed as a messenger of God, and is treated with the esteem of one who has come to deliver a will and heart of God. A dancer also carries that mandate, yet because of spirits of performance and entertainment, and the stigma and perversion of dance in the world, the ministry of dance has often been tainted and watered down to something that fills space in a program. It is the responsibility of the dancer to come against this mentality through intercession, while seeking God for strategies that present tangible revelation that a dancer is also a minister of the word of God and even more so because the dancer is able to physically impart and activate the word God is speaking. Moreover, by carrying the fivefold mantle Jesus gave the church in Ephesians 4, God's purpose for dance can be restored to the His people and the world.

Ephesians 4:11-12 states:

(The Amplified Version)

And His gifts were varied; He Himself appointed and gave men to us, some to be apostles (special messengers), some prophets (inspired preachers and expounders), some evangelists (preachers of the Gospel, traveling missionaries), some pastors (shepherds of His flock) and teachers. His intention was the perfecting and the full equipping of the saints (His consecrated people), that they should do the work of ministering toward building up Christ's body (the church).

The Message Version of verse 7-13 asserts:

But that does not mean you should all look and speak and act the same. Out of the generosity of Christ, each of us is given his own gift. The text for this is, He climbed the high mountain, He captured the enemy and seized the booty, He handed it all out in gifts to the people. Is it not true that the One who climbed up also climbed down, down to the valley of earth? And the One who climbed down is the One who climbed back up, up to highest heaven. He handed out gifts above and below, filled heaven with his gifts, filled earth with his gifts. He handed out gifts of apostle, prophet, evangelist, and pastor-teacher to train Christ's followers in skilled servant work, working within Christ's body, the church, until we're all moving rhythmically and easily with each other, efficient and graceful in response to God's Son, fully mature adults, fully developed within and without, fully alive like Christ.

In order for people to discern our purpose, we must walk in our calling of not just being a dancer, but in the intention to which God gave the earth giftings for the perfecting of the saints and saving lost souls. This purpose is found in the passages in *Ephesians 4* where Jesus said His intention for giving apostles, prophets, evangelists, pastors, and teachers, is that we can mature ourselves and others, while perfecting the things we are maturing in. It is crucial that we embrace this fivefold mandate and go as ambassadors of Christ through these intentions. As dancers, we are not set apart or distinct from this just because we use our bodies to minister the will of God. If anything, we are positioned to be even more effective in bringing to life God's purpose for every given ministry engagement. I declare this because we have the capacity to be the voice of God, and the literal representations of HIM. My God! We are the throne room example made flesh. Yes Lord! We, the dancers, are His word, His breath; His sound waves made flesh. When we minister, we physically demonstrate what God is stating and doing in a particular setting. We are instruments that bring the spirit realm and our invisible God to life. We create and make real and tangible the unseen hope. *Hebrews 11:1, "Now faith is the substance of things hoped for, the evidence of things not seen."* Please understand that I am not saying that all have to have a title or office but Christ has provided a specific mandate through Ephesians 4 that will allow us to be strategically effective when ministering His gospel. His word says that "*He gave some apostles, some prophets, some evangelist (missions), some preachers, and some teachers.*" When Christ gave us as gifts unto the people, He did not expect us to separate ourselves from what He gave depending on the style and method of our ministry. He expected no matter what our style of ministry was, that when we went forth unto the people, we would go under the grace of these positions. These positions are the foundation for ministering effectively in our sphere of influence in that given assignment and are vital to saving souls, perfecting the church and experience heaven in our midst.

I use to attend Christ Temple Global Ministries (CTGM) in Muncie, Indiana. CTGM operates in a fivefold mandate. It was not until 2011 that my leaders shifted me into the office of a *prophet*. Before this recent acknowledgement, I did not profess a title or office. However, being a part of a body where my leader is an *apostle* and because of the calling on my life to which the Lord says I am an *apostle*, the mantle I am sent under fluctuates with each assignment. Please understand that titles help us to categorize who we are, and aides us in asserting authority within our calling, yet the Lord does not need titles to use us in our calling or under a specific fivefold mandate. Let's just take David for example. David was in his early twenties when he was anointed king, but it was at age thirty when he actually shifted into the natural position of reigning as kingdom.

> **1Samuel 16:12-13 denotes:**
> *And he sent, and brought him in. Now he was ruddy, and withal of a beautiful countenance, and goodly to look to. And the LORD said, Arise, anoint him: for this is he. Then Samuel took the horn of oil, and anointed him in the midst of his brethren: and the Spirit of the LORD came upon David from that day forward. So Samuel rose up, and went to Ramah.*

If you study the life of David, you will find that despite initially only possessing the anointing of being king and giftings, God used him wonderfully to bring continuous victory, kingly covering and the establish of heaven to his sphere of influence. David spiritual ruled and governed as king before he naturally was set in the office of king.

Their did come a season, where it was essential for David shift from just operating in just anointing and gifts and talents, to actually naturally ruling and reigning as king over Israel and Judah. Yet despite only having the anointing initially, David operated as king from the moment the Lord revealed to him that this was the destiny he was to possess in life.

2Samuel 5:1-5 reads:
Then came all the tribes of Israel to David unto Hebron, and spake, saying, Behold, we are thy bone and thy flesh. Also in time past, when Saul was king over us, thou wast he that leddest out and broughtest in Israel: and the LORD said to thee, Thou shalt feed my people Israel, and thou shalt be a captain over Israel. So all the elders of Israel came to the king to Hebron; and king David made a league with them in Hebron before the LORD: and they anointed David king over Israel. David was thirty years old when he began to reign, and he reigned forty years. In Hebron he reigned over Judah seven years and six months: and in Jerusalem he reigned thirty and three years over all Israel and Judah.

As God's people, it is very important to be in alignment with the Lord and His timing concerning when we are to shift. Though for whatever reason, we may not possess the title, we should never operate less than what God has called us to be. Because David operated under the anointing and spiritual position of a king despite not holding the position naturally, he was able to reap the benefits of a king for himself, the people and the kingdom of God. David's gift is what made room for him, but it was the calling on his life that brought the fruit of God in his midst. This is what being in alignment with the Lord is all about. This is how we are able to see the fruit of who we are, come to past despite others not recognizing our title, despite religion, tradition, or anything else the world, people or the devil throw our way.

Please know I am not telling you to be rebellious, to defy leadership or go ahead of the timing of God. Yet, I am urging you to come to a place of healing and contentment in who you are in the Lord.

> **2Peter 1:10 encourages us:**
> *Because of this, brethren, be all the more solicitous and eager to make sure (to ratify, to strengthen, to make steadfast) your calling and election; for if you do this, you will never stumble or fall.*

It is essential that we know who we are even if others do not know yet. We gain this information by spending time in the presence of the Lord and seeking His will, direction and calling for our lives. And when He reveals the information to us, we begin to activate it through our giftings and talents. We no longer allow our giftings and talents to define us and we do not even have to go around demanding that others receive what God has said. Yet, we move in the spiritual anointing and grace on our lives, and allow that to not only make room for us, but also reveal and strategically position us into the calling and destiny of God on our lives.

When the Lord uses me in ministry, each engagement is different and depending on what God is requiring me to minister, God may give me to the people in the mandate of an apostle, prophet, evangelist, teacher, or preacher through dance. This may or may not bet true for you, but it is essential as dancers that as we go abroad, we operate and manifest our gift of dance through the initial foundation of the reasons God gave us to the earth. With that focus, the full intentions of His assignment can manifest as effective ministry, and the spirit of performance and entertainment can be crushed and cast out.

Most dancers have more than one gift and are multifaceted in his or her ability to maneuver in and out of the fivefold mandate. I sense that this because of the creativity that is on our lives to create movement. I would moreover, contend that most dancers are intercessors. When we move, we are tilling the ground through intercession. This is how the ground we tread is claimed and depending on which mandate from *Ephesians 4*, we are ministering in at the time, we are making a deposit in the spirit realm that will produce a natural manifestation of the gifts Jesus left the church.

When a dancer goes forth from the context of *Ephesians 4*, his or her ultimate task is to use the strategies that God gives to gain ground and conquer territory for the kingdom.

> **Joshua 1:3 says:**
> *Every place that the sole of your foot shall tread upon, that have I given unto you, as I said unto Moses.*
>
> **Furthermore, Jesus asserted in Luke 10:19:**
> *Behold, I give unto you power to tread on serpents and scorpions, and over all the power of the enemy: and nothing shall by any means hurt you.*

The dancer's main objective is to tread or to move. It does not matter if we are ministering through worship, praise dance, or warfare, every time we move as dancers we are gaining ground in the spirit and natural realms. We are treading and conquering new territories for the kingdom. That is why David said, *"I bless the Lord at all times and his praise shall continually be in my mouth (Psalms 34:1)."*

Merriam-Webster Online Dictionary defines *Bless* as:

1. to hallow or consecrate by religious rite or word
2. to hallow with the sign of the cross
3. to invoke divine care for or health especially to one who has just sneezed
4. praise, glorify; to speak well of, approve
5. to confer prosperity or happiness upon; protect, preserve, endow, favor

King David declares in Psalms 149:1-9:

Praise ye the LORD. Sing unto the LORD a new song, and his praise in the congregation of saints. Let Israel rejoice in him that made him: let the children of Zion be joyful in their King. Let them praise his name in the dance: let them sing praises unto him with the timbrel and harp. For the LORD taketh pleasure in his people: he will beautify the meek with salvation. Let the saints be joyful in glory: let them sing aloud upon their beds. Let the high praises of God be in their mouth, and a two-edged sword in their hand; To execute vengeance upon the heathen, and punishments upon the people; To bind their kings with chains, and their nobles with fetters of iron; To execute upon them the judgment written: this honour have all his saints. Praise ye the LORD.

Verse 5-9 of the Message Version asserts:

Let true lovers break out in praise, sing out from wherever they're sitting, Shout the high praises of God, brandish their swords in the wild sword-dance – A portent of vengeance on the God-defying nations, a signal that punishment's coming, Their kings chained and hauled off to jail, their leaders behind bars for good, The judgment on them carried out to the letter – and all who love God in the seat of honor! Hallelujah!

That word *Execute* in the Hebrew is *Asa* and means to broadly and extremely:

1. accomplish
2. advance
3. appoint
4. become

5. bear
6. bestow
7. bring forth
8. bruise
9. be busy
10. have the charge o
11. commit
12. deal (with)
13. deck
14. displease
15. do
16. exercise
17. fashion
18. hold a feast
19. finish
20. fulfill
21. furnish
22. go about
23. govern
24. hinder
25. be industrious

<u>Merriam Webster's Online Dictionary's definition of *Execute* is as followed:</u>

1. to carry out fully: put completely into effect
2. to do what is provided or required by
3. to put to death especially in compliance with a legal sentence/to put to death deliberately, to punish
4. to make or produce (as a work of art) especially by carrying out a design
5. to perform what is required to give validity to
6. play

7. to perform properly or skillfully the fundamentals of a sport or of a particular play
8. to perform indicated tasks according to encoded instructions
9. to kill, to murder, to enforce

Synonyms for the word *Execute* is as followed:
1. assassin, behead
2. liquidate
3. eliminate
4. electrocute
5. knock off
6. do in, gas
7. bump off
8. put away
9. demolish to death
10. accomplish
11. achieve
12. administrate
13. govern

David understood how movement and his continual blessing of the Lord impacted the spirit and the earth realm. He knew that his praise and worship could not be dependent on how he felt, who was watching and approving, or his circumstances. He seemed to understand that the more he praised and worshipped, the more glory God received, and the more God was able to use him to execute the vengeance and judgment of God, while gaining and establishing new territory in the spirit and the natural realm.

2 Samuel 6:11-1:

And the ark of the LORD continued in the house of Obededom the Gittite three months: and the LORD blessed Obededom, and all his household. And it was told king David, saying, The LORD hath blessed the house of Obededom, and all that pertaineth unto him, because of the ark of God. So David went and brought up the ark of God from the house of Obededom into the city of David with gladness. And it was so, that when they that bare the ark of the LORD had gone six paces, he sacrificed oxen and fatlings. And David danced before the LORD with all his might; and David was girded with a linen ephod. So David and all the house of Israel brought up the ark of the LORD with shouting, and with the sound of the trumpet. And as the ark of the LORD came into the city of David, Michal Saul's daughter looked through a window, and saw king David leaping and dancing before the LORD; and she despised him in her heart.

Earlier in 2*Samuel* we see David and Israel attempting to transport the ark of the Lord into the city of David, but as they were Uzzah touched the presence of the Lord, and God killed him instantly. This made David displeased and fearful so he took the ark of the Lord to Obededom's home where it resided for three months. Before Uzzah died, verse 5 says,

> *And David and all the house of Israel played before the LORD on all manner of instruments made of fir wood, even on harps, and on psalteries, and on timbrels, and on cornets, and on cymbals.*

We can assume that because of the instruments and psalteries and the fact that the word says that Israel played before the Lord, that there was much dancing and rejoicing as the ark of the Lord was being transported. Yet, we see in verse 6 that such powerful dancing and praise and worship, was not enough to spare Uzzah's life. When attempting to prevent it from falling, Uzzah die instantly after touching the ark of the covenant, once the oxen shook it.

> *And when they came to Nachon's threshing floor, Uzzah put forth his hand to the ark of God, and took hold of it; for the oxen shook it. And the anger of the LORD was kindled against Uzzah; and God smote him there for his error; and there he died by the ark of God.*

Israel was offering praises to the Lord, but they lacked intentionality and proper positioning. I say this because in *Exodus 25:14-15*. the word reveals that the ark is to be bared upon the shoulders of priests, nevertheless, Uzzah and Israelites had it on a cart.

> *(The Amplified Version)*
> *And put the poles through the rings on the ark's sides, by which to carry it. The poles shall remain in the rings of the ark; they shall not be removed from it [that the ark be not touched].*

Truly we are carriers, bearers, of the presence of the Lord. We cannot carry it how we desire. We must not only possess the gifts and talents, yet be positionally aligned so that the blessings of God can flow through us. I urge you to consider that when we walk in giftings and talents and we aren't properly positioned before God regarding who we are, how we are to carry His glory and establish His kingdom, we become familiar with the presence of the Lord and this can cause death to us and even to others. Executing vengeance becomes our own demise rather than the demise of the enemy as the very judgment written that Uzzah was supposed to be executing became his own death judgment. It is important to understand that we are not just praise and worshippers, but we are ministers of movement in some fivefold fashion, and we are therefore, called for a specific purpose in executing His vengeance and judgment in the earth.

After hearing that God had blessed Obededom's home and his entire household, David decided to try again to move the ark of the Lord to the city of David. This time, David was determined to honor the Lord at all cost and he was determined to be intentional in governing the presence of the Lord. David and the Israelites therefore, shifted from just being praisers and worshippers (giftings and talents of singing and dancing) to walking in the kingly authority of their calling. When they brought up the ark into the city of gladness this time, David offered a sacrifice every six paces and danced before God with all his might.

2Samuel 6:*12-16:*

So David went and brought up the ark of God from the house of Obededom into the city of David with gladness. And it was so, that when they that bare the ark of the LORD had gone six paces, he sacrificed oxen and fatlings. And David danced before the LORD with all his might; and David was girded with a linen ephod. So David and all the house of Israel brought up the ark of the LORD with shouting, and with the sound of the trumpet. And as the ark of the LORD came into the city of David, Michal Saul's daughter looked through a window, and saw king David leaping and dancing before the LORD; and she despised him in her heart.

That word *Sacrifice* is *Zabah* in the Hebrew is and means:
1. to slaughter an animal (usually in sacrifice)
2. kill
3. to slaughter for eating
4. to slaughter in divine judgment

When considering this definition, sacrifice basically means to execute vengeance, the divine judgment that has been written and established concerning us and God's kingdom. Let's just ponder that for a minute or two.

We like to focus on how David danced with all his might but we never consider the power in David taking six steps to offer a sacrifice....to execute vengeance.

The word *Pace* in the Hebrew is *Sa'ad* and means:
1. step, stride, goings, go
2. steps (of course of life)

Merriam Webster's Online Dictionary defines *Pace* as:
1. rate of movement, especially stepping, walking

2. rate of activity, progress, growth
3. an example to be emulated
4. rate of performance or delivery
5. Any of the various standard linear measures, representing the space naturally measured by the movement of feet walking
6. Distance covered in a step

When David and the Israelites took those six paces they were demonstrating the movement, growth, progress, and advancement of the kingdom of God in the earth. They were using the presence of the Lord to execute the judgment. The number six in the bible is the number of man. We can also break that down even further in that the number five means grace and one is God so David was pursuing the grace and mercy of God every six paces he and the Israelites endeavored. Moreover, man was also created on the sixth day and man was given six days to labor and one day to rest from his works. Thus we can assume David gained revelation that he was called to offer sacrifices of labor that displayed honor and reverence unto the Lord while establish His judgment and rule in the earth. You see it is not about our pretty dances or graceful dance movements, but what is our movement producing, solidifying, in the earth realm? I can dance all day long, but can I take six steps and produce change, execute vengeance, establish judgment in the earth realm?

When David was not offering sacrifices and executing judgment, he was dancing before the Lord with all His might. He was not being familiar or presumptuous before the Lord as they had done previously, or just dancing and performing. David had acquired a revelation that his praise and worship was to be intentional and that as he glorified God, His presence was being established everywhere the soles of His foot tread.

We see even further that David's abandoned worship before the Lord activated and solidified God's Lordship. He also activated and solidified the blessings, judgment, and residence of the presence of the Lord within the land and atmosphere as they traveled.

That word *dance* in this passage of scripture is *Kara* and means to "*whirl.*" When we whirl in the dance, our bodies are acting like planters and we are deeply driving into the ground, everything that God wants to establish while at the same time activating the fruit of that which we are establishing.

Rather than one of them dying as previously occurred when they strived to bring up the ark of the Lord, David's abandoned worship exposed a major stronghold within his own household and that we experience in the body of Christ in general. That was the spirit of Michal. Michal was David's wife and when she saw him dancing before the Lord with all his might, the word says she despised him in his heart.

Verse 13-16:

And David danced before the LORD with all his might; and David was girded with a linen ephod. So David and all the house of Israel brought up the ark of the LORD with shouting, and with the sound of the trumpet. And as the ark of the LORD came into the city of David, Michal Saul's daughter looked through a window, and saw king David leaping and dancing before the LORD; and she despised him in her heart.

Verse 20-23:

Then David returned to bless his household. And Michal the daughter of Saul came out to meet David, and said, How glorious was the king of Israel to day, who uncovered himself to day in the eyes of the handmaids of his servants, as one of the vain fellows shamelessly uncovereth himself! And David said unto Michal, It was before the LORD, which chose me before thy father, and before all his house, to appoint me ruler over the people of the LORD, over Israel: therefore will I play before the LORD. And I will yet be more vile than thus, and will be base in mine own sight: and of the maidservants which thou hast spoken of, of them shall I be had in honour. Therefore Michal the daughter of Saul had no child unto the day of her death.

An essential key to fivefold ministry is that its greatest purpose is for the edifying and perfecting of the saints such that we are all maturing in Christ likeness. When Michal negatively judged David's ministry of dance, he expressed that our call is about glorifying God and building up the people's faith to focus on God through worship and servanthood. This means laying aside titles, honors, personal dignities, perceptions of others, etc., while dismantling self so that God can be honored among all. David knew his call and purpose and let

Michal know that he would be even more vile, as it was God who crowned him and positioned him over the people. He was willing to disrobe himself as king and freely play before God so all knew who really was king. Doing this did not hinder his ability to reign, yet it further established God's ability to reign in and through Him.

David is our most significant prototype as dance ministers of functioning through the ministry mandates Jesus left to the church. I say this because as king he represented the apostle and had a distinct realm of influence that conquered atmospheres and nations while making sure God and His people where edified. He had the heart of a shepherd which is the pastor and desired to see those under him serve and live in the fullness of the Most High God. His Psalms were prophetic and prophesied the coming of the Messiah. He was evangelistic and a teacher in that his lifestyle, Psalms, heart for God, and warfare tactics brought instruction and drew others to serve, praise and worship God. At any given time, David maneuvered in and out of the fivefold mandate with signs following as he won countless wars and conquered the biggest of principalities such as Goliath, Saul and above we see Michal. Throughout his rule, he constantly demonstrated how worship assisted with bringing the kingdom of God into the earth realm. Even with Michal, we see David's dance ministry judge her such that because of her criticism and false judgment, her womb was closed and she never had a child. As dancers, we must be as David and minister through the fivefold mandate, so that we too, can build up the body while dismantling and exposing anything that defies the name and glory of our God.

David could have given into Michal and let her words coward him into being cautious in how He honored God. But even at the expense of his own wife and household, he chose the will and way of the Lord. We must not allow people, emotions, fears, insecurities, or circumstances to dictate our dance ministry. When we are not moving (dancing), no ground is being conquered. When we are not moving (dancing), God is not receiving any glory. When we are not moving (dancing), demonic squatters are possessing our territory, and accepting glory that rightfully belongs to God. We must dance like David danced. We must go as an ambassador with the intentions of changing everything we touch by manifesting ourselves through the fivefold mandate that Jesus placed in us as gifts to the church.

Strategic Fivefold Assignments

It is important to note that no ministry engagement lacks a strategic assignment. Even when we minister at birthday parties, weddings, outdoor services, schools, community functions, pageants, etc., there is a specific reason God is sending us forth.

The word says in Matthew 11:12:
The kingdom of heaven suffers violence and the violent take it by force.

We cannot take the kingdom if we are not moving or going forth to these places with a violent motive to see people saved and set free. There is purpose beyond your cousin inviting you or making a wedding beautiful or the kiddies showcasing their talents" at the praise jam.

Joshua 1:3 states that:
Every place that the sole of your foot shall tread upon, that have I given unto you, as I said unto Moses.

God cannot give us ground in the kingdom if we do not go forth with comprehension that there is a greater purpose than superficial reasons. Most often God will reveal that reason ahead of time in prayer, or through dreams, visions, prophetic utterances, and even through His biblical word. If God sends a minister forth without a specific assignment, then it is for purposes of having that person wholehearted die to self while trusting that when he or she reaches their destination the fullness of who God is will manifest through him or her. This is one way God builds our faith in who He really is and what He can really do through us.

The name of the dance ministry I assist with overseeing at my church is Shekinah Expressions. We minister at churches, birthday parties, weddings, colleges, outdoor services, etc. We always seek to minister through God's purposeful plan and through the operation of the fivefold mandate. We have seen God heal and deliver people at a birthday party and had the DJ asking for prayer. We have seen a person delivered from heroin addiction through ministry at a birthday party. We have had God show up through us at weddings and lives be transformed. We have gone to Baptist churches speaking in tongues and just being us despite the religious bondage, and have been invited back because of the fire of God and the transformation that they received. There have been times that I am saying, "Lord, now you know we are in the strict Baptist house." I am not saying that there aren't any Baptist tongue talkers, but you get my point right? Yet once we start ministering it is all about what He wants. That's all that is important. We can never be less than who He is calling us to be at any given time. We can only go forth in His design so that His will is discernible for all present.

There are times that God will have me accept an engagement where I may not be able to operate in the fullness of the fivefold in the natural realm, whether that be because of denomination, traditionalism, the setting I am ministering in, etc., however, in some form, even if nothing but the dance itself, He will bring forth His purpose for me being there. And because I am walking in His assignment, I am able to respect and gain favor from those I am ministering to and never is the ministry an offense or out of order of what people in their own natural perceptions are seeking to accomplish.

Aside from these instances, I have come to a place in my ministry that if people do not want the fullness of God's strategic plan in me, I simply and politely cannot accept their engagement to come minister in dance. It is vital to let those who invite us to minister know that we do not come to just dance but to minister a word through the arts and that word will come through dance but God may also want to us to share verbally or pray for people as we minister in dance or even afterwards. God may want us to decree and declare and break the atmosphere open before going forth in dance. Or once the dance goes forth, He may want the people to spend time resting or being further delivered through the work He is doing. Only if your spirit is trusted to be free to move by the Holy Spirit will you be able to accept the engagement.

There will be times you will have to decline engagements because people do not have this vision of dance ministry or they are not willing to allow the Holy Spirit to dictate their program. But remember you are not entertainment. You are a minister in the dance. And because you use your body as a representation of God and are a speaking being, you come as the sum instrument of Him. When you go forth in the dance, you go forth as a total representation of God, and it is essential that you are allowed to be free to share all He is requiring through that assignment. For the church to grasp this vision of dance, we must be fervent intercessors against spirits of resistance, religion, tradition, entertainment, performance and we must steer way from using the world's perception of dance in our ministry. We must be willing to be totally separated from anything that will appear to contaminate and construe our ministry with the world's counterfeit of dance and we must help people see dance as a ministry by first grasping a full understanding of dance ourselves, seeking God for strategies, and not allowing people to make us performers and entertainers when God is sending us forth to do a work through a particular ministry engagement.

Fivefold Operations

Let's explore the fivefold positions and how operating in the fivefold edifies the body, while shifting atmospheres and people, thus bringing forth the presence and wonders of God.

Ephesians 4:11-12 states:

(The Amplified Version)

And His gifts were varied; He Himself appointed and gave men to us, some to be apostles (special messengers), some prophets (inspired preachers and expounders), some evangelists (preachers of the Gospel, traveling missionaries), some pastors (shepherds of His flock) and teachers. His intention was the perfecting and the full equipping of the saints (His consecrated people), that they should do the work of ministering toward building up Christ's body (the church).

(The Message Version)

He handed out gifts above and below, filled heaven with his gifts, filled earth with his gifts. He handed out gifts of apostle, prophet, evangelist, and pastor-teacher to train Christ's followers in skilled servant work, working within Christ's body, the church, until we're all moving rhythmically and easily with each other, efficient and graceful in response to God's Son, fully mature adults, fully developed within and without, fully alive like Christ.

APOSTOLIC DANCE MINISTRY

Apostle in the Greek is *Apostolos* and means:

1. a delegate, messenger, one sent forth with orders
2. specifically applied to the twelve apostles of Christ
3. in a broader sense applied to other eminent Christian teachers
   1) of Barnabas
   2) of Timothy and Silvanus

Merriam Webster's Online Dictionary defines *Delegate* as:

1. a person acting for another
2. a representative to a convention or conference
3. a representative of a United States territory in the House of Representatives
4. a member of the lower house of the legislature

When going forth under the apostolic mandate you are presiding in the position of a delegator. A delegator is one who goes in the place of another and is a representation of a judicial government that presides over a group of people, nation, state, etc. So essentially, when moving in the apostolic, you are acquiring orders from the Lord and are going forth in His stead; as His voice and heart, with specific orders to bring His kingdom (government) to pass within the people and/or within that environment.

Because an apostle or one under this mandate is going forth as a representation of the Lord, he or she operates as one of dominion, strategically assigned to shift people and/or a particular area to another dimension and influence in the Lord. Dominion is ultimate authority that is unstoppable. Thus, when operating apostolically, one is specifically assigned a kingly realm of dominion and influence.

Often, we are taught that an apostle or one who operates apostolically is one who starts churches, church movements, or ministries such as mission's movements, dance ministries, etc. This is indeed true, yet the apostolic mandate is not limited to just establishing churches and the like. The apostolic mandate:

- Is one of influence in the spirit and natural realm beyond where the people are and even sometimes beyond where you are spiritually.

- Is a "knowing" that "this is my assignment" and a level of fearlessness that comes with it.

- Though you may be in your room or before the people ministering in dance, when under an apostolic anointing one is often inside the spirit realm. It is like you know you are dancing in your room or before the people but it feels like you are inside a bubble or floating above or inside the power and presence of God. I believe this is the dominion that protects and gives influence to the person in this position.

- Commands the attention of its congregation, the demonic and the spiritual realm.

- Possesses authority and power that shifts lives, churches, communities, and/or atmospheres.

- Is one of dominion and prominence; demons and opposition may occur, but will have no success over one who is walking in the apostolic.

- Declares the voice and judgment of God that plant and establishes His will in the spirit and/or natural realm. Most often God will give a specific assignment and one will know what they are planting or establishing.

- Sets a standard for excellence and creates followers of Jesus Christ.

- Shifts believers to higher realms of understanding, belief and inspiration.

- Identifies gifts via the power of God and the presence that takes over an atmosphere

- Has the ability to birth revival in a church or region.

- Breaks down religious and traditional walls and barriers.

- Brings burdens for nations.

- Dismantle chief, territorial, and ancient spirits and pull down principalities that may have a city, community, church, or people bound.
    - Chief spirits are stronghold demons that rule and have rank in the demonic kingdom and hold people in bondage to the enemy.
    - Territorial spirits rule over specific geographical locations, such as poverty spirit ruling in poor communities.
    - A principality is when demon princes rule over states, cities or nations.

In *Acts 16,* Paul and Silas were beaten and thrown in jail for delivering a sorcerer and preaching Jesus.

Verse 16-23:
And it came to pass, as we went to prayer, a certain damsel possessed with a spirit of divination met us, which brought her masters much gain by soothsaying: The same followed Paul and us, and cried, saying, These men are the servants of the most high God, which shew unto us the way of salvation. And this did she many days. But Paul, being grieved, turned and said to the spirit, I command thee in the name of Jesus Christ to come out of her. And he came out the same hour. And when her masters saw that the hope of their gains was gone, they caught Paul and Silas, and drew them into the marketplace unto the rulers. And brought them to the magistrates, saying, these men, being Jews, do exceedingly trouble our city, And teach customs, which

are not lawful for us to receive, neither to observe, being Romans. And the multitude rose up together against them: and the magistrates rent off their clothes, and commanded to beat them. And when they had laid many stripes upon them, they cast them into prison, charging the jailor to keep them safely:

Paul and Silas were under an apostolic mandate to establish the kingdom of God in that city. They were coming against the laws by preaching Jesus and were establishing God's law in the people and in the sphere of influence. Their workings were so evident that a soothsayer possessed with a spirit of divination acknowledged that they were men of The Most High God.

The word *Divination* the Greek is *Python* and means:

1. in Greek mythology, the name of the Pythian serpent or dragon that dwelt in the region of Pytho at the foot of Parnassus in Phocis, and was said to have guarded the oracle at Delphi and been slain by Apollo
2. a spirit of divination

This was a major principality of idolatry operating in that area. Those participating in divination would go to the soothsayer and pay money to receive psychic words concerning their lives. Paul displaced this principality by casting it out of the damsel. This made her masters upset and they brought Paul and Silas before the courts and had them beaten and thrown in jail.

Paul and Silas where naturally bonded, but spiritually they were still free to rule in dominion and authority as representatives of the Most High God.

Acts 16:26-34 reads:
And at midnight Paul and Silas prayed, and sang praises unto God: and the prisoners heard them. And suddenly there was a great earthquake, so that the foundations of the prison were shaken: and immediately all the doors were opened, and every one's bands were loosed. And the keeper of the prison awaking out of his sleep, and seeing the prison doors open, he drew out his sword, and would have killed himself, supposing that the prisoners had been fled. But Paul cried with a loud voice, saying, Do thyself no harm: for we are all here. Then he called for a light, and sprang in, and came trembling, and fell down before Paul and Silas, and brought them out, and said, Sirs, what must I do to be saved? And they said, Believe on the Lord Jesus Christ, and thou shalt be saved, and thy house. And they spake unto him the word of the Lord, and to all that were in his house, and he took them the same hour of the night, and washed their stripes; and was baptized, he and all his, straightway. And when he had brought them into his house, he set meat before them, and rejoiced, believing in God with all his house.

Paul and Silas were apostolic sent ones. Therefore, when they went forth in prayer, and praise, it affected the atmosphere such that a great earthquake occurred and the foundations of the prison were shaken. These signs were a spiritual shifting was taking place and naturally manifesting itself within the prison. This was because God was bringing judgment for them being imprisoned, while making it clear that He had all dominion in that area. Paul and Silas prayer and praise also delivered the people that were bound in prison. The word says that the prison doors opened and the bands where loosed. God had changed their position in the spirit realm and it thus manifested by the doors of their natural prisons being opened and them being freed from bondage. The reaction of such a move of God brought fear to the point of considering suicide rather than facing God. Yet God's desire is always initially to save so Paul let the guard know all was well. Thus, the guard and his entire household was saved and baptized.

Examples of Apostolic songs that can be ministered in dance are "Psalms 27" by *Shekinah Glory Ministries,* "We Speak to Nations" by *Lakewood Church.*

PROPHETIC DANCE MINISTRY

Richard A Murphy wrote an article in 1998 called "Worship in Dance," and suggested that Israel viewed dance as a prophetic gift because during Miriam's time, dance, music, and instruments was taught in the school of prophets. The bible never records one prophecy of Miriam, yet she was known in biblical history as a prophetess and for leading the Israelites in this celebration of dance. Though the dance Miriam led was not what we would exactly consider prophetic today,

The Hebrew root word for *Dance* is *"Machashabah"* which means:

1. thought
2. device
3. invention

This suggests that the processional of the dance was strategic in nature and impacted the atmosphere and future of the people and the climate much like prophetic dance today. At an even greater stretch, it could be suggested then that this first law of dance that Prophetess Miriam led was apostolic as it celebrated the defeat of a national military force of elite troops that truly was the drowning of a principality. This great procession of triumph that Prophetess Miriam led included singing and the use of the timbrel; the timbrel is representative of striking, to beat, to smite or kill. She was in spiritual warfare.

Timbrel is the same Hebrew root word as *"Tabering." Tabering* means to beat the breast which can include forms of dance as spiritual warfare and intercession. So though naturally Prophetess Miriam was leading a dance of celebration, perhaps in the spirit realm she was completing and solidifying within the supernatural what had already occurred in the natural realm. Though Israel wondered in the wilderness for forty years, their fate within the slavery of Egypt was over from that day forward.

When considering another facet of prophetic dance, in *Luke 1:28-41*, we find the angel of the Lord revealing to the virgin Mary that she will have a child by the name of Jesus. To confirm this word the angel tells Mary that her cousin Elizabeth who was once barren is pregnant as well. After the angel departs, Mary visits Elizabeth. Upon arrival the scripture states the following:

> **Luke 1:39-41:**
> *And Mary arose in those days, and went into the hill country with haste, into a city of Juda; And entered into the house of Zacharias, and saluted Elisabeth. And it came to pass, that, when Elisabeth heard the salutation of Mary, the babe leaped in her womb; and Elisabeth was filled with the Holy Ghost: And she spake out with a loud voice, and said, Blessed art thou among women, and blessed is the fruit of thy womb. And whence is this to me, that the mother of my Lord should come to me?*

The word *Lead* is *Skirtaō* in the Greek and means:

1. to skip
2. to jump
3. sympathetically move (as the quickening of a fetus)
4. leap
5. leap for joy

The leaping of the baby was a prophetic act that birthed forth the Holy Spirit in Elizabeth, and she begin to prophecy a blessing while confirming the angel's word to Mary that she was the carrier of the savior, Jesus Christ. Elizabeth spoke further that the leaping of the baby in her womb was in response to hearing her salute. She expressed further of how there shall be a display of what the angel had shared with Mary. It was as if the leap of the babe was a prophetic activation of the performances of that word coming to past in May's life.

Verse 42-45:
And she spake out with a loud voice, and said, Blessed art thou among women, and blessed is the fruit of thy womb. And whence is this to me, that the mother of my Lord should come to me? For, lo, as soon as the voice of thy salutation sounded in mine ears, the babe leaped in my womb for joy. And blessed is she that believed: for there shall be a performance of those things which were told her from the Lord.

Prophetic Dance

- Is ministered with regard to the sensitivity to the leading of the Holy Spirit and the atmosphere. A person should be submitted to leadership and respect the decisions of leadership, especially during congregational worship.

- Opens the spirit realm - the heavenlies. Capable of manifesting a fresh wind and zeal for God into the atmosphere.

- Is from the Father to a person, group of persons, or a congregation.

- A dance that may bring forth a fresh atmosphere of the anointing and the glory of God.

- Often spoken in first person as if God is talking through the dancer and having the dancer interpret what He is saying through dance

- One of confirmation concerning present and future situations.

- One that may encompass a word of knowledge or may visually interpret specific information about a person or church and situations and circumstances that may be presently occurring; will occur in the future or may have already occurred in the past.

- Imparts visual stimuli in a person's life, church, or community that provides comfort, exaltation and/or hope to hold on to the promises of God.

- Many that are in the office of a prophet may dance words of correction and caution and may also receive dances that provide visual examples of what is occurring in the spirit realm. Those that are being used prophetically may not be given this level of assignment and most often will minister dances that encourage, exalt and comfort.

Ministering Prophetic Dance

- A dancer may minister prophetically with music playing while he or she interprets the music.

- A dance can also interpret the scriptures through prophetic dance. Someone can read the scriptures and the dance can interpret the passage through dance and dramatization.

- Someone may prophecy and the dancer can interpret the prophecy.

- God can give a person or even the dancer a song and then the dancer can dance to it.

- Often in congregational worship a prophetic song will come forth. God may unction the dancer to begin prophetically and/or spontaneously ministering in dance to that song.

- The song does not necessarily have to be a prophetic song. It can be a song that is being ministered. God can give a person a vision of a dance or even a dramatization to that song and unction the person to minister it to a person or congregation.
- Sometimes when praying for people, God may unction a person to minister

movements that represent pulling down strongholds and/or breaking bondages off people. God may give a person a dance that brings healing and peace. He may have the person minister specific movements around the person to demonstrate his covering, protection or love. God may even have a person dance with another person. When I have ministered in this fashion, it was to bring another level of freedom or joy in a specific area of a person's life.

- Some prophetic dances are at times choreographed. Not all prophetic dances are spontaneous. God will provide the dancer with a choreographed piece or even one that is to be ministered prophetically to people. An example of this type of prophetic dance would be "Yes" by *Shekinah Glory Ministries* or "No Limits" by *Israel and New Breed.*

Examples of prophetic dances that may be ministered are "Lord of the Breakthrough" and "It's Raining" by *Israel and New Breed,* "Contact" and "Burning One" by *Joann McFadden.*

EVANGELISTIC DANCE MINISTRY

Evangelistic dances bring a message of conviction that draw people to Christ with hope and faith that God is the deliverer, healer, savior, and answer to their every situation. We see this within the story of the prodigal son who returned home after squandering his inheritance.

> **Luke 15:25-32:**
> *Now his elder son was in the field: and as he came and drew nigh to the house, he heard musick and dancing. And he called one of the servants, and asked what these things meant. And he said unto him, Thy brother is come; and thy father hath killed the fatted calf, because he hath received him safe and sound. And he was angry, and would not go in: therefore came his father out, and intreated him. And he answering said to his father, Lo, these many years do I serve thee, neither transgressed I at any time thy commandment: and yet thou never gavest me a kid, that I might make merry with my friends: But as soon as this thy son was come, which hath devoured thy living with harlots, thou hast killed for him the fatted calf. And he said unto him, Son, thou art ever with me, and all that I have is thine. It was meet that we should make merry, and be glad: for this thy brother was dead, and is alive again; and was lost, and is found.*

An evangelistic anointing can also instill a desire to dance within the heart of the people as they are renewed and revived in the promises and strength of God and filled with faith to believe in Him and to trust His love for them yet again.

Psalms 30:11 reads:
Thou hast turned for me my mourning into dancing: thou hast put off my sackcloth, and girded me with gladness;

(The Message Version)
You did it: you changed wild lament into whirling dance; You ripped off my black mourning band and decked me with wildflowers.

Psalms 149:3 declares:
Let them praise his name in the dance: let them sing praises unto him with the timbrel and harp.

Psalm 150:4 also declares:
Praise him with the timbrel and dance: praise him with stringed instruments and organs.

The word *Dance* in these scriptures is the Hebrew word *Machol* and means:

1. round dance
2. chorus
3. dancing

This type of dancing denotes celebration and unity, to which one who ministers as an Evangelist, operates in to release among people, communities, etc.

Evangelistic Dance

- Shares the good news of the gospel while seeking to save souls; focuses on the salvation of the person by introducing people to Christ, ministering the love of God for his people, and ministers salvation.

- Provokes change in the inner man, and moves people from soul to spirit, from focusing on circumstances to focusing on God.

- Strives to unify people and atmospheres with God and with one another, and brings messages of hope, encouragement, and joy.

- Demonstrates feet shod with the preparation of the gospel of peace and the good news of the gospel.

- Evangelism touches individuals, families, communities, and nations with an anointing that brings life changes.

Examples of evangelistic dances that may be ministered are "I Need You to Survive" by *Juanita Bynum* and "Never Would Have Made It" by *Marvin Sapp.*

Luke 10:21 contends:

In that hour Jesus rejoiced in spirit, and said, I thank thee, O Father, Lord of heaven and earth, that thou hast hid these things from the wise and prudent, and hast revealed them unto babes: even so, Father; for so it seemed good in thy sight.

(The Amplified Version)

In that same hour He rejoiced and gloried in the Holy Spirit and said, I thank You, Father, Lord of heaven and earth, that You have concealed these things [relating to salvation] from the wise and understanding and learned, and revealed them to babes (the childish, unskilled, and untaught). Yes, Father, for such was Your gracious will and choice and good pleasure.

In this passage of scripture, we find Jesus rejoicing.

Rejoice in the Greek is *Agalliao* and means:

1. to exult
2. rejoice exceedingly
3. be exceeding glad

The root Greek word for *Rejoice* is *Hallomai* and means:

1. to leap
2. to spring up
3. gush up
4. of water

Now Jesus was not doing a choreographed dance but I can imagine Him jumping up and down and praising the Lord and just doing His dance steps unto the Lord. The fact that Jesus rejoiced in the dance should encourage us to embrace the ministry of dance and become free praise and worshippers before the Lord. Jesus states that there are some things related to salvation that has been hidden from those who perceive themselves as intelligent but are revealed to those who are humbled...babes before the Lord. We definitely know that though dance has always been a biblical custom, it hasn't necessarily been utilized among the body of Christ in fullness and has at times, been a hidden weapon within the kingdom. Lately we see God releasing His ministers of dance as never before and they are coming forth in great fashion that reveals powerful revelations and fruit of the kingdom. Those who operate in a pastoral call or assignment of dance are revealers of the concealed wonders of God's word and kingdom. They seek to bring maturity within the believer and draw them to a greater place of revelation and depth in the Lord.

Pastoral Dance

- Reveal the mysteries of God's word and kingdom.
- Feed the sheep of God.
- Provides biblical principles to build faith and maturity.

- Provides a specific message that feeds the soul and spirit of the people and imparts revelation of who Christ is to us and our reasoning for being saved.

- Yields a biblical impartation and most often would have some form of prophetic and apostolic connotation as it would be difficult to go under this mantle only since pastors are generally called to specific flocks of people.

    - Sometimes the dancer's movements are ministering a message from the pulpit and is often ministered directly to people.

- Has a heart of compassion; seeks to cover, protect and guard the people.

- Provides some facet of covering for the people who are receiving from it.

- Seeks to lead, set the example, and minister messages of care and concern for the people.

Examples of pastoral dances that may be ministered are "I Won't Go Back" and "I Give Myself Away" by *William McDowell.*

TEACHING DANCE MINISTRY

David is our greatest example of one who teaches others how to minister in dance and in leading others to dance before the Lord. We already discussed *Exodus 15:20*, where Prophetess Miriam was leading the congregation in a celebration dance after Pharaoh and his army drowned in the red sea. In addition to what her dance already revealed, by leading the congregation, she was also teaching others how to properly celebrate victories and spiritually solidify and establish the natural victory that had taken place.

Exodus 15:20:
And Miriam the prophetess, the sister of Aaron, took a timbrel in her hand; and all the women went out after her with timbrels and with dances.

Psalm 9:13-14:
Have mercy upon me, O LORD; consider my trouble which I suffer of them that hate me, thou that liftest me up from the gates of death: That I may show forth all thy praise in the gates of the daughter of Zion: I will rejoice in thy salvation.

Ecclesiastics 3 states:
A time to weep and a time to laugh, a time to mourn and a time to dance;

The word *Time* denotes that dance itself has its set aside place among us and that though it can be spontaneous, because there is a set time, we can even have those occasions where we make preparation to dance.

Verse 10-11 reads:

He hath made everything beautiful in his time: also he hath set the world in their heart, so that no man can find out the work that God maketh from the beginning to the end.

(The Amplified Version)

He has made everything beautiful in its time. He also has planted eternity in men's hearts and minds [a divinely implanted sense of a purpose working through the ages which nothing under the sun but God alone can satisfy], yet so that men cannot find out what God has done from the beginning to the end.

The word says that everything is beautiful in its time. We can consider then that when dance is executed in its proper time, it displays the beauty and the will of the Lord. Those who operate as a teacher of dance, have the wisdom to display the heart and movement of God in His timing and even to teach others how to dance for and unto the glory of the Lord, the end of *Ecclesiastes* states that there is nothing new under the sun. Dance is not new to the Lord. We see that even as He listed it in this chapter, He embraces it and He created it to be an important part of who we are.

Teaching Dances

- Teaches and ministers the movement of God and the types of movements of God.
- Ministers fundamental principles of the Word.

- Ministers biblical principles of praise and worship, warfare and the biblical bases of dancing before God and ministering dance.

- Minister's dances may provide visualizations of how to come out of bondages or how to go higher in God or may teach the people a particular characteristic of God.

- This type of dance can also be one of demonstration and dramatization, where groups are used to demonstrate scriptures, life issues, and provide admiration and hope.

- Sometimes provides messages of instruction in the music and song through dance.

- Elevates understanding of spiritual matters.

Ministering Teaching Dances

- God may have a person teach a dance to a church or group setting.

- Maybe instead of ministering a dance a person will teach it and then lead the people in ministering the dance unto the Lord.

- Sometimes before ministering a dance, the Lord may have a person to teach on dance by sharing scriptures about dance and the call of dance to provide a foundation that can break down religious walls and ideas and open the spirit realm for dance being seen as a ministry in a particular church setting.

- Or maybe a person will be the lead of a dance ministry or teach dance in the community or at a conference, etc.

"Glorious" by *Martha Munizzi or* "The Presence of the Lord is Here!" by *Byron Cage* can be ministered to a congregation or group setting. In our dance ministry, we often minister "Bow Down" by *Paul Morton,* and we will have someone representing how to overcome bondage and totally submitting in bowing and worshipping God.

Creating a Fivefold Team Within the Dance Ministry

Often within a ministry, the leader completes most of the tasks within that ministry. He or she choreographs the dances, oversee the finances, book the engagements, pray and impart into the members, and on and on. As a ministry grows and even as the leader matures personally, these duties can become cumbersome and wear on leaders to the extent that the anointing and power of the dance ministry weakens and/or the enemy is given open doors to wreak havoc within the group.

True fivefold ministry is about teamwork. It is also about releasing people into their perspective callings so that the body of Christ can continue to extend and grow such that the lineage of the covenant God made with Abraham concerning making his descendants as numerous as the stars in the sky could manifest eternally *(Exodus 32:13)*. The word says,

Ephesians 4:11-12 states:
(The Amplified Version)
And His gifts were varied; He Himself appointed and gave men to us, some to be apostles (special messengers), some prophets (inspired preachers and expounders), some evangelists (preachers of the Gospel, traveling missionaries), some pastors (shepherds of His flock) and teachers. His intention was the perfecting and the full equipping of the saints (His consecrated people), that they should do the work of ministering

toward building up Christ's body (the church).

(KJV)
Verse 11-13
And he gave some, apostles; and some, prophets; and some, evangelists; and some, pastors and teachers; For the perfecting of the saints, for the work of the ministry, for the edifying of the body of Christ; Till we all come in the unity of the faith, and of the knowledge of the Son of God, unto a perfect man, unto the measure of the stature of the fulness of Christ:

Edifying in the Greek is *Oikodomē* and means:

1. edify, edifying, edification
2. (the act of) building
3. building up
4. the act of one who promotes another's growth in Christian wisdom, piety, happiness, holiness

I am not sure how the body of Christ veered away from the thought of teamwork and providing avenues where spiritual lineage could progress, yet often the responsibilities of a ministry is placed on one person who is striving to birth a vision, work a vision and keep it alive. As a result, many ministries are in constant turmoil or strife, lack a spirit of excellence due to weariness or burnout, are controlled by religion, legalisms, or the ministry ends up miscarrying the vision or blatantly aborted. Insecure leaders feel threatened by their position or someone doing the job better than them so they operate in a spirit of pride and demonic control in effort to keep members submitted and from going forth in their own personal ministries.

In these passages of scriptures, we discern that one person did not do it all or possess it all. We can assert that multiple members are to operate in different genres such that a complete work can prevail in perfecting and fully equipping the saints personally, and the body of Christ as a whole. Furthermore, we can also conclude that true leadership is about edifying, building up, promoting others beyond self, lacking personal agendas, and that teamwork is essential for setting a standard in who we are as the body of Christ.

With this being considered, I want to note that true fivefold ministry is about imparting, releasing, and establishing. It is about creating avenues so that people can not only grow and be utilized in their giftings, but can come into a true personal understanding of who they are in God and who He is in them, while operating in a tangible manifestation of the calling and destiny on their lives. This manifests by allowing group members to have a voice and say so within the group, sharing the duties of the group with them so they are taking responsibility and ownership of carrying the vision of the ministry, and creating avenues for them to be activated in who they are in the Lord personally and who they are within the group as a whole.

The word says in Philippians 3:1-5:

(The Amplified Version)

So by whatever [appeal to you there is in our mutual dwelling in Christ, by whatever] strengthening and consoling and encouraging [our relationship] in Him [affords], by whatever persuasive incentive there is in love, by whatever participation in the [Holy] Spirit [we share], and by whatever depth of affection and compassionate sympathy, Fill up and complete my joy by living in harmony and being of the same mind and one in purpose, having the same love, being in full accord and of one harmonious mind and intention. Do nothing from factional motives [through contentiousness, strife, selfishness, or for unworthy ends] or prompted by conceit and empty arrogance. Instead, in the true spirit of humility (lowliness of mind) let each regard the others as better than and superior to himself [thinking more highly of one another than you do of yourselves]. Let each of you esteem and look upon and be concerned for not [merely] his own interests, but also each for the interests of others. Let this same attitude and purpose and [humble] mind be in you which was in Christ Jesus: [Let Him be your example in humility:]

(New Living Translation)
Is there any encouragement from belonging to Christ? Any comfort from his love? Any fellowship together in the Spirit? Are your hearts tender and compassionate? Then make me truly happy by agreeing wholeheartedly with each other, loving one another, and working together with one mind and purpose. Do not be selfish; do not try to impress others. Be humble, thinking of others as better than yourselves. Do not look out only for your own interests, but take an interest in others, too. You must have the same attitude that Christ Jesus had.

(KJV)

> *If there be therefore any consolation in Christ, if any comfort of love, if any fellowship of the Spirit, if any bowels and mercies, fulfil ye my joy, that ye be likeminded, having the same love, being of one accord, of one mind, Let nothing be done through strife or vainglory; but in lowliness of mind let each esteem other better than themselves, look not every man on his own things, but every man also on the things of others, Let this mind be in you, which was also in Christ Jesus.*

The word *Vainglory* in the Greek is *Kenodoxia* and means:

1. empty glorying
2. self-conceit
3. vain glory
4. groundless
5. self esteem
6. empty pride
7. vain opinion
8. error

The word says we are to esteem and support others higher than we would ourselves. That as we encourage one another in love, compassion and fellowship, it promotes like-mindedness and unity. However, when we do not possess or operate in these attributes we give way to contention and vainglory. Strife breeds contention, discord and division. Vainglory produces an empty glory, self-conceit, groundless which means lacking foundation, empty pride (false sense of security), puffed up opinions and risk operating in error.

When reading further in this chapter, the word says that even Jesus humbled himself unto the Lord and because of this, God exalted His name above all the universe (*Philippians 2:10-11*).

> **<u>Verses 14-18 state:</u>**
> *(The Amplified Version)*
> *Do all things without grumbling and faultfinding and complaining [against God] and questioning and doubting [among yourselves], That you may show yourselves to be blameless and guileless, innocent and uncontaminated, children of God without blemish (faultless, unrebukable) in the midst of a crooked and wicked generation [spiritually perverted and perverse], among whom you are seen as bright lights (stars or beacons shining out clearly) in the [dark] world, Holding out [to it] and offering [to all men] the Word of Life, so that in the day of Christ I may have something of which exultantly to rejoice and glory in that I did not run my race in vain or spend my labor to no purpose. Even if [my lifeblood] must be poured out as a libation on the sacrificial offering of your faith [to God], still I am glad [to do it] and congratulate you all on [your share in] it. And you also in like manner be glad and congratulate me on [my share in] it.*

<u>The word *Vain* in that scripture is *Kenos* and means:</u>

1. empty (literally or figuratively): in vain, vain things
2. devoid of truth
3. of places, vessels, etc. which contain nothing
4. of men that are empty handed, without a gift

5. destitute of spiritual wealth, of one who boasts of his faith as a transcendent possession, yet is without the fruits of faith
6. of endeavors, labors, acts, which result in nothing, vain, fruitless, without effect, vain of no purpose

Paul was teaching the people the importance and benefits of esteeming and sowing into others spiritually. He expressed that if this occurs, then what he has imparted into the leader demonstrates its purpose, and the work that they complete will also exude purpose. And that this purpose would allow the people to be set apart while being lights and examples to the world, and will produce a greater glory for the person on the day when Jesus returns to claim the body of Christ.

Paul further conveys that vainness separates a person from the truth of the Lord, causes one to do a whole bunch of work that produces no fruit, and causes spiritual destitution in the leader's life and those he or she oversee and are to be lights for. He then demonstrates the importance of esteeming by validating and appreciating the sacrifices that are being made for the sake of the gospel and encourages them to do the same for him. Paul was thus expressing the strength of teamwork and unity and whether leading or following, how we all are essential to the work of the Lord.

As God has been working in and on me regarding the qualities of a good fivefold ministry leader, I have learned that true leadership is having the ability to impart into others in a manner that creates a spiritual extension and lineage of who you are in the Lord and who He is in you. It is not about doing all the duties and Lording over people. True effective leadership encompasses the fruit and character of God through a spirit of excellence, while strengthening such that God's kingdom can advance and be eternally established in the earth realm.

A good leader has the ability to:

- Exude Godly character
- Esteem and encourage others in purity or without any hidden motives
- Pursues the eyes, ears and heart of Christ; see a person and the ministry beyond where they are and for who they are, and esteem, teach, impart, activate, and help process them out to that place
- Discerns and prays concerning the group members' personal calling in Christ and provide avenues for them to operate in the calling
- Lead and follow
- Delegate duties based on callings and step back and allow the person/persons to operate in that assignment while giving grace for mistakes made and constructive criticism that helps them progress forward in healthiness
- Shift members from a mindset of not just being utilized in giftings and talents but understanding and cultivating the calling and full destiny on the person's life
- Effectively communicate with all types of people and even to explore difficult issues, even if it is issues the group/member has with the leader or a decision a leader makes

- Be sensitive to the personal issues of group members and can decipher when deliverance and healing issues necessary for assisting that person is progressing towards healthy maturity in the Lord
- Effectively communicate, inspire, motivate and give clear/sound direction or at least motivate and encourage others to invests in the vision even if the fullness of it has been revealed
- Seeks to be spiritually and emotionally healthy by constantly striving to improve self and creates avenues to improve others
- Comfortable with making mistakes and admiring them while realigning self and the ministry with correcting what has been wrong
- Repents quickly, solves personal issues in a healthy and timely manner and does not allow personal challenges to affect his or her communication with others or the ability to adequately lead the group
- Maintain balance between ministry and personal life; discerns when to rest and refresh ones' self and the group
- Fear God not man and allows God to be the source of his or her strength, success, and promotion
- Is humble, confident, and mature in the things of the Lord
- Has a sense of humor; can laugh at self, Satan, and in the face of adversity

- Be faithful to the services and visions of the church and faithful in seeing the vision of God come to past within the group
- Does not mind praying and fasting and sacrificing time, self, and desires for the good of the ministry
- Creative, inventive, and ambitious; passionate for the things and people of God
- Be honest, fair in judgment; pursues the eyes and will of the Lord so that His will can be established in people, situations, and environment
- Extends grace without holding grudges, harboring, resentment or unforgiveness
- Assertive, competent, confident, courageous, bold when necessary, and forthright
- Open to allowing God to be free to move without building high places on areas of success, yet trusting that God can do above and beyond one's last or previous success
- Flexible, open to change and operating in the timing and movement of the Lord
- Remain rooted and grounded in the word, pursues and operates in the truth of the Lord
- Pursues the fullness of the Holy Spirit and gifts of the spirit operating in his or her life or ministry

As director of our church's dance ministry, for years I completed most of the tasks for our dance ministry. Let me just share a few in hopes of enlightening your eyes to realizing that as leaders, everything we do may appear to be God and even naturally beneficial, but is not the Lord or spiritually fruitful. I choreographed the dances, chose the songs we were to minister and sought the

Lord concerning the purpose of the ministry engagements. I booked the ministry engagements and collaborated and consulted with those we were ministering for as needed, prayed for all the members, led the practices, provided transportation for members to and from practices/engagements, taught and imparted into the members, prepared, checked and responded to the homework assignments, collected and managed the dues, made the uniform purchases and for a while washed, kept them at my home, packed them and lugged them to engagements when we had to minister. I would be at practice early to work with members who needed further assistance, cleaned up after members when practice was over, after engagements, locked up the church and on and on. Our ministry ministers every Sunday morning during praise and worship in addition to taking ministering engagements within and outside the church so it truly is like operating two ministries in one. The challenge with all these duties however, is that it caused constant cycles of burnout, and I would go through seasons of resenting God, the ministry, the group members, and questioning if I even wanted to be a leader or in ministry all together.

Several years ago, the Lord begins to deal with me about delegating more responsibilities out to the group. He also released revelation on how to shift the mindset of group members from that of just a dancer, but exploring what their calling and destiny was, and activating and utilizing that within the ministry. I begin to delegate most of the duties that I mentioned above out to group members which gave them more ownership in helping to carry the vision and responsibilities of the ministry.

In addition, I stopped engaging group members according to their style of dance. By style I mean whether they were mime, jazz, ballet, hip hop dancers, etc. I also ceased with engaging them based on whether they felt they were praisers, worshippers, intercessors, warfare dancers, etc., as truly all dancers should flow in each facet of these giftings. I in turn, begin to activate their mind based on where they felt God desired to use them within the fivefold ministry and I begin to focus on whether they sensed they were prophetic, evangelistic, pastoral, etc., or even eclectic in nature, and I begin to teach them how to operate in the fullness of their calling based what their positions were within the fivefold ministry I did this not just as it relates to dance but who they were in general. This provided them the opportunity to grow not just in dance as it relates to fivefold ministry, but the fullness of the calling on their lives. For example, if a member states that she feels she has been called in the area of the prophetic, I will use her in practice to search out what the Lord is saying for the group. As we are praying and preparing for practices I will ask her if she sees, feels or hears anything the Lord may be saying. I will activate her calling in other ways by encouraging her to speak what she feels God is saying to group members or for ministry engagements we are preparing for and even encourage her to seek God for a word for the church or the people we are ministering to. If God reveals to us that we are minister a prophetic dance, then I will assign her to assist with choosing the song and assisting with the choreography. This shifts the group member from operating in the gifting of dance to cultivating their calling in the prophetic. It also activates the group at a greater level in the area of fivefold ministry, especially when all the group members are operating from their perspective callings. We are thus able to bring a greater perfection of the ministry the word speaks of in Ephesians, because we have the components of pastoring, evangelizing, teaching, prophesying, and establishing through the apostolic manifesting. It also allows us to flow together as a team where everyone is being utilized in their perspective callings and grace. Members are also able to flow in and out of the fivefold positions as God leads, and because they are able to gleam from the anointing on one another's lives through impartation, and just through the mere fact that this is alive within the womb and atmosphere of the ministry. Therefore, each member is receiving revelation, knowledge and impartation within each area of the fivefold. And when we go forth in ministry, we are able to release complete fivefold ministry and full establishment of God's heavenly kingdom to the services, programs, people, and atmospheres that we are ministering in.

Another notion the Lord has impressed upon me to do with our ministry is to set up a schedule, where each month a different member oversees the ministry, while I assist them. This person is responsible for overseeing practices, assisting with choreographing for ministry engagements and searching out what the Lord desires us to minister. They help pray for members and the group during practices, choosing garments, etc. Basically, they lead the group as I would as the primary leader. This allows the person to grow in the area of leadership and develop their skills in the area of their calling as they lead through who they are in God, and the ministry is allowed to gleam from that perspective. The person also oversees the dancers during Sunday morning praise and worship. They are responsible for seeking the Lord concerning what He desires to do in the people and/or atmosphere, what strongholds to combat if necessary, and what weapons, tools, movements, etc., to use so that God's presence and wonders can invade and be established in a greater way.

As you have read this section, I encourage you to truly seek the Lord on how you can assist with shifting your dance ministry into a true fivefold ministry team. Ask God to give you a strategy and vision for what that entails as it relates to you personally, those who are a part of the dance ministry, and the mandate and call on the group as a whole. Shifting members and the group to a place of calling rather than just operating in dance ministry, releases a greater anointing and power on the group and allows the ministry to be more effective in fulfilling the assignments God has granted to your hands. It also opens the doors for the ministry to be utilized in other areas. I state this because, when our team takes engagements, we often do not just dance but we are provided grace to release a word to the church or people, pray for people, and operate in other areas of our calling. It is therefore as if dance was the avenue that opened the door to ministry, but the fullness of who we are personally and as a group is allowed to be activated as we go forth in ministry. When are then not just seen as dancers but ministers of the heart and movement of God that is able to bring forth the fullness of His kingdom.

Combating Religion and Tradition

Religion & Tradition

Two of the main spirits that have tried to keep dance out of the church and strives to immobilize the ministry when it goes forth are the spirits of religion and tradition. I despise these spirits. I look for them, and they look for me. The supernatural truth about these two spirits is that they cannot be reasoned with, and one cannot attempt to combat them with natural logic. Both these spirits believe they are right in all facets and hold the purest truth of what holiness is and what the standards are for holy living. But the truth about these spirits are that they box God and people into set standards of living that leave little room for the Holy Spirit to teach, guide and fully operate in one's life, church, community, and within the kingdom as a whole. These spirits are kingdom racism fashioned as Christianity as they provide systems and hierarchies that leaves others standing by the way side that cannot live up to the standards imposed through its doctrine. Religion and tradition will not give up its need to be right, and though these spirits know the Bible and use it for its standard of living, it twists principles to bind people into a set way of thinking and living. The only way to combat these spirits is to come against them in the spirit realm.

To avoid yielding to religious or traditional paradigms, it is essential to refuse to box God, self, or experiences into one frame of mind or principle. Every assignment must be allowed to have its own unique experience.

God must be sought and allowed to lead each opportunity so that His will can be manifested. **The moment we try to recreate something God has already done in our lives or ministry, we create a high place and open the door to religion and tradition.** The moment we ostracize and reject people because they do not fit into our mold of thinking or living, or live up to our perceived standards of holiness, we risk falling into religious and traditional doctrines. In ministry, these are the biggest challengers of a dancer and these spirits seek to keep us standing on the outside of Jesus Christ. The devil is defeated liar!

We serve a supernatural God that cannot be boxed in to our standards of living and manifesting. At times, religion and tradition work very subtle. It will sneak into one's life and church through culture and customs that really are pagan and worldly. An example of this would be holidays such as Christmas, Easter, Martin Luther King Jr. Day. Then there is the blatant religion and tradition that strives to kill the move of the Holy Spirit. For example, putting programs on time agendas so the Holy Spirit cannot move freely, taking the arts out the church. These strongholds will at times embrace the arts to an extent but will use them in the perspective performance and entertainment so that God gets no glory, as then they are perceived worldly, and thus the perception that they do not belong in the church is strengthened.

One manner I am discerning lately among the church body, is that these strongholds are allowing the Holy Spirit to move to a certain extinct and even miracles, signs, and wonders are manifesting, but one will see the wall of these spirits manifest as soon as he or she does something that is contrary to the hidden norm, hidden rules and doctrines that these spirits possess. Even though dance and the arts are now being allowed more freely, rarely is that dancer provided the platform to operate in fullness of his or her calling.

In the natural it appears that these strongholds are not in operation because of its manipulation of giving the heavens the opportunity to move. This manipulation seems as if the free presence of God is operating. The reality of these spirits is seen, felt, and experienced only through a spiritual eye. These spirits will allow just enough presence of God in to make people think they are walking in the fullness of Him, but not enough where the satiating presence of God can operate in totality in the natural realm. I would even go as far as to declare that you can often times discern when these spirits are in operation when the presence of God lacks consistent fruit of His kingdom life. The word says, "*Thy kingdom come, Thy will be done on earth as it is in heaven" (Matthew 6:10).*" It is not enough just to feel God or experience His presence. Our lives and ministries should be transformed in His likeness. If this is not occurring, then there is a possibility that there is a form of godliness, religion and tradition still in operation in the spirit realm.

Please understand that I am not saying we should not have standards of living. These standards, however, should not infringe upon God and His movements in and through us. Because of His presence being active in us, we should be demonstrators of His character and fruit. We should also exhibit compassion to see people operate in and receive from Him even at the cost of our own doctrines. I would like to think the soul has two standards of living and that is heaven or hell. Jesus came to save the lost. He knew our souls were going to hell, and He came to save us. Jesus never compromised His values, but He never lost compassion to consider the soul of man. We should have that same mindset. When we lose sight of this, and allow our laws and values to close our heart from having compassion for the soul, we allow the operation of religion and tradition to enter into our lives, homes, and community. When that happens, we close the doors for people to be free in their expressions of who God is in them. This is what keeps dance *chillin'* on the outside of ministry instead of penetrating the midst of it. Dancers and the ministers of the arts in general, must understand that religion and tradition are our primary enemies because we possess the ability to counterattack them in the spirit realm through movement, thus enabling more spiritual freedom to manifest on earth. We are a unique representation of God, and we are a radical portion of His Spirit that cause the freedom of His will to operate without boundary to the spirit or the natural realm. The very presence of the arts provides an opportunity for religion and tradition to be defeated, and for the true glory of God and the will of His kingdom to manifest consistently in our lives, churches, ministries, and communities.

Merriam-Webster's Online Dictionary defines *Religion* as:

1. the state of a religious
2. the service and worship of God or the supernatural
3. commitment or devotion to religious faith or observance
4. a personal set or institutionalized system of religious attitudes, beliefs, and practices
   scrupulous conformity
5. conscientious
6. a cause, principle, or system of beliefs held to with ardor and faith

Tradition is defined as:

1. an inherited, established, or customary pattern of thought, action, or behavior
2. a belief or story or a body of beliefs or stories relating to the past that are commonly accepted as historical though not verifiable
3. the handing down of information, beliefs, and customs by word of mouth or by example from one generation to another without written instruction
4. cultural continuity in social attitudes, customs, and institutions
   characteristic manner, method, or style

Discerning Religious Operations

Religion suffocates the presence and fruit of God in people's lives and within atmospheres of churches. When God's plan goes forth, religion will seek to divide people from God's work by using legalism, privilege, status, and strict standards of living, principles and protocols. Often the person God is using to do His work experiences a sense of resistance or blatant rejection. A wall will literally go up in the spirit realm and naturally it appears as if you are standing outside of the situation looking in, even though in reality you are a part of the situation. Sometimes naturally I can see a fog or veil between myself and the people. It is as if they are seeing what God is doing, but there is no response to it. It appears as though they are watching a movie and though the movie is good, they are totally separated in their emotions and spirits. Therefore, the movie may have a message, but the message does not pierce their spirits because they are disconnected from the effects of it. That is what religion does within an atmosphere. It will close the people off from experiencing the full effect of God's plan. It will be like watching God at work and just like a movie, they will be in awe of some of the things that will manifest, but nothing will be planted in their spirits. The ministry will not manifest change or transformation in the lives of the people, the church and/or the atmosphere.

The reason this occurs is because religion has separated the person and the congregation on standards of legalism and privilege that can only be received from people of its class. This is also why sometimes ministry will go forth and no one will receive it, but another will go forth and bring the same message and everyone will start shouting and running around the church. Religion has the tendency to operate with a respect of person's agenda, which shuts out the true will of God. It also operates in a form of godliness that lacks conviction and change.

Romans 2:8 assert:
For there is no respect of persons with God.

Within the body and amongst ministries in the church, religion tends to operate by separating churches and ministries via spirits of division, so that we can be at odds with one another. The fullness of God's principles of us being all one body with different members will not operate

Romans 12:4 read:
For as we have many members in one body, and all members have not the same office.

Churches will exist within miles, blocks of one another and never fellowship because of differences in denomination, race, or perceived, "we are the only holy ones" status. When religion is in operation within the spirit realm of a church, ministries tend to be separated from one another, and difficulty with bring ministries together when necessary will arise. There at times, is an absence of fellowship between ministries. Those who step out the box and fellowship with those who are a part of other ministries will experience discord, back biting and rejection. Each ministry will believe "the glory comes through them," and will not deem it necessary to work with other groups. Though the members themselves may not believe this, what is going on within the spirit realm manifests this perception in the natural. Remember religion operates behind the scenes, and therefore it is important that when we start to see these things manifest, that we come against religion in the spirit realm. Unity among the fine arts within a church is the vital key for snuffing out the religious spirit and bringing the fullness of God to pass in peoples' lives, church services and communities, climates, nations, etc. Fine arts ministry provides endless opportunities for the impossibilities of God to manifest with unwavering uniqueness. The arts ministry restores giftings that the devil has tainted through the world's perversion to the church, so that the souls of people can be reached and saved regardless of age, ethnicity, gender, language, culture, trend, etc.

Discerning Traditional Operations

Tradition operates by binding the life of a person and or a church to set methods operating that have been passed through the generations. No matter how much a person or church has the desire and potential to move forward, tradition will hold them to past standards and cause them to perform within those parameters.

When going abroad to minister, I usually can discern the operation of religion and tradition in an atmosphere of a church because there is a barricade of resistance which usually presents itself as judgment or refusal to receive. Sometimes a church will be free to a degree as these spirits may not possess it, but will oppress it, and one will see the things I stated earlier in operation. One can also usually discern these spirits as there will be a sense of heaviness in the atmosphere, and your spirit may feel heavy or grieved. In effort to combat these spirits, it is essential to minister what God desires. It is also important that every move is designed and lead by Him, as each dance and move has a spiritual meaning and plan attached to it. God's moves are designed to combat fortresses, pull down strongholds, and breakthrough barriers, so that His people can possess the liberty of the land, sphere of influence and blessings that He has ordained for them. This is also the reason it is essential that as dancers, we spend time with God and let Him choreograph the movements. Every move is spiritually definitive. You may not know what the moves are doing, but God does. When you display the movement and breathe of God in your dance, you are able to beat these strongholds down in the spirit and natural realm.

There will be times when you will practice a dance one way and when you go to minister, God will change every move. When this happens do not fight against what God is doing through you, flow with Him. What you did in your personal time may have been necessary and vital to what God was going to do when you went forth to minister. It may have tilled the ground for His ultimate workings to come forth. The more time you spend with God the more sensitive you are to the spirit and are able to discern His methods and be uncovered to His will.

Demonic Attacks Against Dancers

Because a dancer has minimal time minister, it is important to remain in a place spiritually to hear God's voice and receive His strategies and moves for a dance. This allows God's message and assignment to manifest with signs following. It also prevents the ministry from being consumed by performance, entertainment, traditionalism and religion.

Sometimes the dance is not always about the people you are ministering directly to. It could be about that community, territory, the spiritual atmosphere of that church or even a personal bout that ministry is encountering. Therefore, it is important not to get caught up in the people's response or lack of response to your dance selection. If you did God's will, there will be a peace and conclusion in your spirit. Focusing on the crowd's response and letting that dictate your ministry can open the door to pride, haughtiness and/or insecurity. It can also draw a dancer away from the assignment of God because he or she is so focused on self and how he or she is being viewed, rather than God's purpose for the assignment.

Some dancers even tend to go through the motions of a ministry piece and consciously disconnect from the crowd and the atmosphere when they feel the crowd is not receiving. It is as if they are dancing within themselves as to hide from rejection, and are doing just enough to get the ministry piece over with. The dancer could also struggle with low self-esteem or low self-worth, and these challenges manifest themselves when going forth in the ministry of dance. Especially in areas where a dancer does not quite possess the faith to trust that it is not about them dancing, but is about the Holy Spirit is dancing through them.

Every assignment has purpose and most often that purpose is not about us. When we disconnect from the assignment, we have made God's work be about us and the realization of such behavior is that we have exalted self, pride, and ego (haughtiness), or our own fears and insecurities above God's will for that assignment. Seeking God's will for ministry disciplines our focus, enmeshes us with compassion and obedience, and provides us with clear understanding that every assignment has a distinct clear purpose that has nothing to do with the people's reception of us or our ministry.

Below is a list of attributes indispensable for remaining grounded and focused and effectively ministering the assignment at hand.

- Self-confidence
- Holy Ghost boldness
- Surety of who you are in God and who He is to you and in you
- Understand your calling
- Confidence that the dance that is in your spirit is a present truth for the people

- A daily pursuit for wholeness and righteousness; a heart of repentance & willingness to be processed to wholeness despite past or present circumstances

    - **1 Timothy 6:11 -** *But thou, O man of God, flee these things; and follow after righteousness, godliness, faith, love, patience, meekness.*

- The fruit of the spirit & agape love because dancers cannot minister judging the congregation or audience

    - **Galatians 5:22:23 -** *But the fruit of the Spirit is love, joy, peace, longsuffering, gentleness, goodness, faith, meekness, temperance: against such there is no law.*

- The ability to manifest the rhema word through your body

- A love for the essentials - worshipping, praising, praying, fasting, reading the word

David possessed these attributes. The bible says that David was a man after God's own heart. David did not lack sin, however, he never let sin rule in his life. He was constantly in hot pursuit of the deeper and greater things of God. And when he fell sort, he would seek God with graved repentance in hopes of restoring his place with God.

God is not looking for us to be perfect. If we were perfect, we would not need a perfect God. He is looking for someone who is willing to be processed into perfection. He is seeking those who are refusing to reign with sin, but reign with Him in purity. This is what enabled David to dance naked before the ark and the people of Israel, even though he was king, and even though at times he fell short of God's glory. He had a boldness that said, "I am running hard after God and I do not care who is watching, who sees me naked for Him, who does not like it, and who is going to shun me for it." Even when his wife ridiculed him, he did not back down from whom he knew himself to be or who God was to Him.

2 Samuel 6:14-23:
And David danced before the LORD with all his might; and David was girded with a linen ephod. So David and all the house of Israel brought up the ark of the LORD with shouting, and with the sound of the trumpet. And as the ark of the LORD came into the city of David, Michal Saul's daughter looked through a window, and saw king David leaping and dancing before the LORD; and she despised him in her heart. Then David returned to bless his household. And Michal the daughter of Saul came out to meet David, and said, How glorious was the king of Israel to day, who uncovered himself to day in the eyes of the handmaids of his servants, as one of the vain fellows shamelessly uncovereth himself! And David said unto Michal, It was before the LORD, which chose me before thy father, and before all his house, to appoint me ruler over the people of the LORD, over Israel: therefore will

I play before the LORD. And I will yet be more vile than thus, and will be base in mine own sight: and of the maidservants which thou hast spoken of, of them shall I be had in honour. Therefore Michal the daughter of Saul had no child unto the day of her death.

All throughout the Psalms, we see David repent with sorrow before God. He dealt with his issues with depth and in honesty through His relationship with the Lord, which enabled him to be free from shame, guilt, condemnation, and unresolved issues when he came before the people.

Psalms 51:1-13:

Have mercy upon me, O God, according to thy lovingkindness: according unto the multitude of thy tender mercies blot out my transgressions. Wash me throughly from mine iniquity, and cleanse me from my sin. For I acknowledge my transgressions: and my sin is ever before me. Against thee, thee only, have I sinned, and done this evil in thy sight: that thou mightest be justified when thou speakest, and be clear when thou judgest. Behold, I was shapen in iniquity; and in sin did my mother conceive me. Behold, thou desirest truth in the inward parts: and in the hidden part thou shalt make me to know wisdom. Purge me with hyssop, and I shall be clean: wash me, and I shall be whiter than snow. Make me to hear joy and gladness; that the bones which thou hast broken may rejoice. Hide thy face from my sins, and blot out all mine iniquities. Create in me a clean heart, O God; and renew a right spirit within me. Cast me not away from thy presence; and take not thy holy spirit from me.

Restore unto me the joy of thy salvation; and uphold me with thy free spirit. Then will I teach transgressors thy ways; and sinners shall be converted unto thee.

In this passage of scripture, we see David acknowledging that he has sinned and needs restoration with the Lord. David states that he desires truth in his inward parts...in the deep places of his being. This is generally how David approached God throughout his walk and even at times when God had to call him out on some matters, such as Nathan confronting David about adultery with Bathsheba in *2Samuel 12*, David would become transparent before the Lord so that God could replenish, restore and even renew him. This is the reason David was favored of the Lord. He was a man after God's very own heart.

Often people will know they are called to minister in dance, but will have minimal understanding of who they are personally and have not dealt with underlying personal issues which causes these areas to manifest in their ministry before the people. When we have low-self-esteem, condemnation, shame, guilt, fear, and/or have unresolved issues that we aren't dealing with before God, this prevents us from connecting with the audience and often shame, guilt, fear and shyness, tends to rule our dance instead of the Holy Spirit. We often look down or in the sky rather than at the audience. Our moves will be timid and restricted and lack the power of God. And our spirit man is hindered from uniting to those we are ministering too. When the Holy Spirit is not in charge, people tend to connect out of issues and at times no connection with the people will occur. This will cause the message of God to be lost or aborted, because the people are receiving an impartation through our soul and soul issues, rather than the purity of the spirit of God within us. It is essential to work on our character, personality, and issues so that we can receive healing in our souls and be supernaturally empowered such that our spirit man rules and lead our lives. This enables us to be effective ministers that render God's assignment with boldness and fervor.

The word says that when David committed adultery with Bathsheba, it purified her from her uncleanness.

> **2Samuel 11:3-4:**
> *And David sent and enquired after the woman. And one said, Is not this Bathsheba, the daughter of Eliam, the wife of Uriah the Hittite? And David sent messengers, and took her; and she came in unto him, and he lay with her; for she was purified from her uncleanness: and she returned unto her house.*

Merriam Webster's Online Dictionary defines *Uncleanness* as:

1. morally or spiritually impure
2. infected with a harmful supernatural contagion
3. prohibited by ritual law for use or contact
4. dirty, filthy
5. lacking in clarity and precision of conception or execution

This is what sexual sin, perversion, and witchcraft, does to our bodies. It makes what was pure about us dirty, filthy, supernaturally contagious, such that whatever is unclean within us is spewed into the atmosphere when we go before the people in ministry. We like to think that people do not see our sin and many do not have a clue what we have done in secret, but the word says that *"no flesh can glory in the presence of God" (1Corinthians 1:29)*. Because the presence of God is so pure, it exposes the lust and sin within us, which results in our dance manifesting sexually and sensually. In such instances, we are unable to control our body movements, and our dance mimics sensual movements, and the seductiveness of the world.

As saved people, we are the first to say that others, especially men should not be enticed by our dance. And this is indeed true, but when we go forth with sexual sin in our spirits, it can indeed cause others to sway from God. The bible says that when the daughter of Herodias danced before the King, he was so pleased that he promised to give her whatever she desired. She asked for John the Baptist head and though he was sorry for having sworn to give her whatever she asked, to keep face before the people, he had John the Baptist beheaded.

Mark 6: 21-26 reads:
And when a convenient day was come, that Herod on his birthday made a supper to his lords, high captains, and chief estates of Galilee; And when the daughter of the said Herodias came in, and danced, and pleased Herod and them that sat with him, the king said unto the damsel, Ask of me whatsoever thou wilt, and I will give it thee. And he sware unto her, Whatsoever thou

> *shalt ask of me, I will give it thee, unto the half of my kingdom. And she went forth, and said unto her mother, What shall I ask? And she said, The head of John the Baptist. And she came in straightway with haste unto the king, and asked, saying, I will that thou give me by and by in a charger the head of John the Baptist. And the king was exceeding sorry; yet for his oath's sake, and for their sakes which sat with him, he would not reject her.*

We are responsible for what we put into the atmosphere. Because dance ministry is visual and people tend to be more effected by what they can see, we have the power to transform lives as well as sway them. We also have the power to change people' perceptions about dance, as well as, feed into the stigmas that have been passed down regarding dance ministry. It is essential to make sure we are not willingly participating in sin and that we keep a heart of repentance before God, so that our ministry can go forth with power and might that draws people to God instead of away from Him.

Sometimes, it okay to have butterflies before you minister, however, nervousness should never become anxiousness or fear. The butterflies remind us that we cannot minister in our own strength and that it is necessary to lean on God so that His will goes forth in fullness. However, when we are experiencing anxiousness or fear, this is not of God; especially when we feel tormented to the point of not wanting to minister or clamming up before the people. The word says, *"God has not given us a spirit of fear; but of love, and of power, and of a sound mind (2Timothy 1:7).* Even with butterflies, we should be able to remain focused on God's assignment and go forth with soundness and power.

Let's break the ministry of dance down more in relations to spirit, body and soul.

Spirit *(The spirit consists of the Holy Ghost and will of God)*
When His spirit rules the dance, God's will and fruit manifest.

Body *(The body consists of the Flesh, Self & Ego)*
When flesh rule in the dance, it tends to manifest as arrogance, boastfulness, perversion, lust, sensuality, and or a lack of control particularly in movement. Movements may appear carnal, worldly, egotistical and sometimes wild as if the person is in another zone.

When self or the personality rule, it manifests as fear, shame, condemnation, shyness, insecurity, haughtiness.

Soul *(The soul consists Emotions & Heart Issues)*
When emotions rule the dance, emotions tends to manifest as hype posing as anointing.
Heart issues tend to exude that there are personal issues going on in your life. It tends to show that you aren't really in a place of stability in your life at that particular time.

SIDEBAR: A born again person cannot be demonically possessed in their spirit but can be in their body and soul. Some strongholds in our lives are not always about a demonic possession as it could simply be behavior patterns that need to be broken or spiritual maturity and stability that need to be acquired in certain areas. One can often discern spirits or curses are at work in their lives/ dance, when there is a difficulty in gaining freedom in that area. If a spirit or curse is present, there is always and underlying reason. Do not cast spirits out without first dealing with the issues, otherwise the demonic spirits will just return stronger. Overcoming the underlying problem illegalizes spirits and brings about true eternal freedom.

Demonic Spirits that Attack Dance Teams

Competition, jealousy, and discord create disunity within ministries and can literally destroy them. Often people are unaware that they have or are participating in the operation of these spirits until they are in the heat of the battle. This it because the conflict starts with subtle words and gestures, yet the more they marinate within the mind, heart and atmosphere, the greater their main purpose expose itself in an obvious manner. These spirits strengthen when there is a lack of communication or miscommunication between those involved and the root of them is often a personal insecurity and/or inadequacy. Moreover, these spirits feed and have the potential to draw those with similar issues, and can often cause opposing teams within a group to operate through unresolved issues and delusional truths that have been puffed up by insinuating conversations and crafty implanting of negative thoughts. The initial instigator will often have a victim mentality and have a difficult time accepting responsibility or acknowledging for his or her actions in giving way to these spirits to operate in or through him or her. It is therefore, essential to pray and approach such situations from a spiritual rather than personal aspect in order to break down this mindset, and bring about resolution/deliverance from the effects of these spirits.

Everyone in your ministry is not going to like one another. God does not require this of us, however, His word does encourage us to:

- Show ourselves friendly *(Proverbs 18:24)*
- To esteem one another higher than ourselves (*Philippians 2:3*)
- To love one another (*John 15:12*)
- Love is a big one as it was one of Jesus commandments
  - *A new commandment I give unto you, That ye love one another; as I have loved you, that ye also love one another* (*John 13:35*).

1Corinthians 12:4-8 states:
Love suffers long and is kind; love does not envy; love does not parade itself, is not puffed up; does not behave rudely, does not seek its own, is not provoked, thinks no evil; does not rejoice in iniquity, but rejoices in the truth; bears all things, believes all things, hopes all things, endures all things. Love never fails…" Therefore, if you are really loving someone it brings about a godly respect and compassionate understanding even if you do not like them or care for them personally. This is what Jesus had and what enabled Him to die for the salvation of people who persecuted Him.

In addition to requiring members to love and respect one another, it is important that leaders teach the dance ministry effective relationship/communication skills. One of my pet peeves about the church is we get people saved but then they relate to one another how they did in the world; particularly, because they aren't taught basic skills to let them know otherwise. Then when people are released into various ministries, we expect them to get along just because they are saved; and they do, at least until someone strikes a nerve/unresolved issue and starts reminding them of their bossy momma, or controlling boyfriend that beat them. Then the defenses surface, chaos starts, and the cycles from the world begin. This is the reason many backslide, or never really acquire the fullness of living for God. Many lack the necessary tools and healing needed to transform into the healthiness of the Lord.

In ministry, we must know and demonstrate good communication skills and to express our feelings properly, even when we are receiving or providing information that may step on toes or may not be easy to hear. As leaders, it is important to also allow our members to express themselves to us. This should be done in private and even if you do not agree, present an environment that allows the person to feel heard while setting some solutions in place to either work on or resolve the matter. Moreover, teach your members to discern when what they are really upset about is not you or others, but a past unresolved issue, and provide them with skills to be able to walk in ministry and still work on personal bouts. I communicate to my group that we are all working out our salvation in some area, and as long as we walk in the flesh, there will be always something God will be working out of us. Our walk with Jesus is not about being perfect but allowing God to perfect us. The best way to bring unity to a group is to keep the lines of communication open, even if that means sitting done with everyone individually and collectively and hashing out issues. Also, teaching your group members healthy relationship skills and how to walk with God without letting past and present circumstances exalt above Him combats against unity as well. It is also important to counterattack disunity in the spirit realm by canceling seeds of discord, competition, jealousy, and continuously decreeing unity over your group and the lives of each member.

Some group members are seasonal. Not everyone is there to stay and not everyone is there to minister in dance. Some are sent by God to receive an impartation from the group and then they move on. Sometimes this can be through the ministry of dance and sometimes it is through participating in other areas within the dance ministry. A lot of times, seasoned people will stay too long and God will allow discord to remove them. And let's just be honest and admit that some people are sent by the devil. You will know them and must be honest with yourself about who they are so that you spiritually cover yourself, the ministry and the other members. I know we do not like to believe the devil is among us or is sent to dwell among us, I am sure God felt the same way when he had to kick Satan out of heaven and heaven was a holy place, but such people are sent to spy out the ministry and/or to wreak havoc for purposes of sowing discord, destroying the ministry, getting members off focus so God's work become secondary, and/or to bring weariness upon the group and leader so that they cannot minister effectively.

Each dance ministry has a specific mandated assignment within the heavenlies and only those God ordained will be a part of that mandate. Of course, it is awesome when a bunch of people are ministering in dance before God. When you have such visions but lack the numbers, borrow ministers from other dance groups or off the pews. Never be so focused on wanting a huge group that you allow people in or to stay that are not a part of God's plan for that ministry. Some people may have a call to dance, but not meant to be a part of a group. There should be a plan within the church that allows these persons to be utilized and submitted in their gifting without having them be a part of a ministry that God has not called them too. When people are made to be a part of a ministry that God has not ordained, it opens the door for discord and drama.

Another way to combat disunity is not to allow others to speak things into your ministry by saying one dancer is better than the other or making inferences that one dancer is "more anointed than the other." Each group member has their own style of dance and anointing. And depending on the ministry piece and calling, does something different in the spirit realm. There natural talents will dictate the anointing, call and assignment. Though the choreographed movements of the dance are in sync, they all move differently and are doing different things supernaturally. When an army is marching, they all are in sequence; they are chanting the same thing and marching to the same beat. Their footing and hand movements are in unison, and they may even move their weapons the same, but when they enter the war zone, they all fall into distinct positions and each component is necessary to combat the enemy and to protect one another against the enemy. A dance ministry and any ministry for that matter is the same way. The word says we all have different members but are of the same body *(1 Corinthians 12:12).* Do not let people sow seeds of pride and discord by making subtle comparisons between group members and leaders reframe from this as well. When others participate in such behavior, rebuke it immediately via prayer, otherwise you will see the seed grow with members comparing themselves one to another and putting others down who they deem "less anointed." Members will begin to walk in hesitancy, insecurity and/or fear with no definitive root cause. This is because of remarks like this being sown into your ministry. Always esteem your group and group members personally and uniformly, especially when you see areas of growth. And always stress that you are a team and everyone has their own unique calling and gifting that makes that group whole, and is essential for each assignment progressing effectively.

Ways to bring about total freedom in the ministry of dance is studying God's word, fast, pray and spend time soaking in the presence of God.

Dance and God's Word

I cannot say enough about having a biblical foundation for every ministry engagement. When God gives me an assignment, I usually search the word for a biblical foundation for the strategies He has given me. Sometimes I verbally declare these scriptures daily until it is time to minister. Our dance ministry completes homework for most of our engagements or have a focus of some sort they are to pray concerning or contend for. These assignments usually include scriptures, personal questions that they may need to work on or we as a group need to work on to prepare ourselves for the ministry. Homework assignments improve, strengthen and fortify us so that further revelation of the strategic assignment God can manifest. By reading our word and studying to show ourselves approved through homework assignments, we become the strategy. It takes on life within us and if we never open our mouths to say, *"thus said the Lord,"* our ministry of dance speaks His voice with clear volumes. Our dance team has had little to no training and we do not profess to be the greatest of dancers as most often the moves God gives us are simple in nature. His force in us is the key to making His will come to past in our lives. The word is the breath, the *"Ruach"* of God. There is nothing like having God's breath blow in and through you. I must state again, I cannot say enough about having a biblical foundation for every ministry engagement.

There are instances where God may not desire a dance piece per say, but for your ministry to dance the scriptures. We do this at times when the scripture goes forth on Sunday mornings. This brings the scriptures to life before the congregation and awakens the atmosphere for greater praise and worship to go forth unto God. One of the ways I minister the scripture at home is to recite a set of scriptures daily for a while until I start to memorize them without reading. As I am able to recite them from memory, I dance them while declaring them into the atmosphere. I would also recommend making the scripture personal. As you declare the Word in a personal manner by using pronouns of *I, Me, Us,* etc., it brings about greater revelation and breathes the reality of the scripture into your existence. In addition, this enables your recall to be greater when striving to breathe God's word into your daily situations.

Fasting

It is a typical facet in dance ministry that in effort to control flesh during ministry is to dance in a stiff lethargic style of movement. This is generally in effort to keep from being an offense and manifesting sensual and worldly movements. Earlier I stated that the only way to gain territory and give God glory was to move or to tread. One must dance and accentuate movements that do not limit God and His Holy Spirit or diminish His power and perfection of gifting. Dancing lethargically not only diminishes who God is, but diminishes your testimony of being delivered and free in Him. In addition, it does not effectively minister the assignment at hand, and aside from fear of bringing worldly dances in the church, lethargic ministry is one of the main reason that dance ministry has had a difficult time being received in the church.

Answers.com. defines *Fasting* as:

1. To abstain from food.
2. To eat very little or abstain from certain foods, especially as a religious discipline.
3. The act or practice of abstaining from or eating very little food.
4. A period of such abstention or self-denial.

From the fourth definition, we can discern that fasting is not just about abstinence from food, but any pleasure that requires discipline. Refraining from food along with other pleasures such as TV, support systems that will normally be a voice in your life, the internet, entertaining or recreational activities, etc., increases the productivity of one's fasts, and makes God's voice and fruit strong and mighty in one's life.

When the disciples could not cast the demonic spirit out of the child, Jesus said to them, *"This kind can come forth by nothing, but by prayer and fasting" (Mark 9:29).* Please let me express that this is one of those kinds. Dance is one of those ministries where fasting is essential in killing the flesh so that freedom in movement can occur. It is an established spiritual principle that *flesh cannot glory in the presence of God (1Corinthians 1:19).* Flesh is exposed under the anointing as the *gifts are without repentance* (*Romans 11:9*), so if there is anything in our flesh, even the religion operating through lethargic movements, it will show itself. Fasting is the only method of killing the flesh and making sure it submits to the will and presence of God. Fasting will also bring about a physical freedom that will allow one to move more freely with an increased precision and grace that radiates from your flesh being dead, naked and shameless before God.

> **Timothy 5:3 maintain:**
> *And the very God of peace sanctify you wholly; and I pray God your whole spirit and soul and body be preserved blameless unto the coming of our Lord Jesus Christ.*

Praying

Praying allows us inside the heart and mind of God through intimate communion with Him. This is the best way to get to know God and His strategies. This is also a great way to get to know ourselves and what needs to be changed in us so that we can be more like Him. And ultimately, in God's presence is where the anointing lies.

It is not just a cliché to declare that it is the anointing that breaks yokes and sends demons fleeing.

> **Isaiah 10:27 declares:**
> *And it shall come to pass in that day, [that] his burden shall be taken away from off thy shoulder, and his yoke from off thy neck, and the yoke shall be destroyed because of the anointing.*

Without the anointing a dancer is no different than a worldly entertainer. One can have technique and all the right moves, but if there is a lack in the anointing, no lives or atmospheres are changed, no ground is taken, no glory is given unto God, and really the person is simply filling up space in a program. It is the anointing that puts the finishing touches on our movements. The anointing is what sounds the alarm in declaration that ground is being taken. It is the anointing that set a part ministry from performance, and gives off light that the All Mighty God is being glorified.

Soaking in the Secret Place

Sometimes I love to just sit or lie quietly and love on God or provoke His presence by asking Him to hang out with me. I may rest quietly or worship within myself until I feel His presence soaking me, absorbing me, saturating my very essence. Sometimes, I will get up and dance in His soaking glory or I may lay and sit quietly while continuing to rest within Him. Resting in God is where total submission, as well as the power of the ministry of dance, as well as our calling resides. If a person wants power to protrude his or her dance, one must make the biblical word flesh, but getting inside of His glory. The only way to do this is to spend time resting and being totally vulnerable before God, and allow Him to soak, absorb and thrust him or her into the power of His glory.

John 15:4-8 states:

(The Amplified Version)

Dwell in Me, and I will dwell in you. [Live in Me, and I will live in you.] Just as no branch can bear fruit of itself without abiding in (being vitally united to) the vine, neither can you bear fruit unless you abide in Me. I am the Vine; you are the branches. Whoever lives in Me and I in him bears much (abundant) fruit. However, apart from Me [cut off from vital union with Me] you can do nothing. If a person does not dwell in Me, he is thrown out like a [broken-off] branch, and withers; such branches are gathered up and thrown into the fire, and they are burned. If you live in Me [abide vitally united to Me] and My words remain in you and continue to live in your hearts, ask whatever you will, and it shall be done for you. When you bear (produce) much fruit, My Father is honored and glorified, and you show and prove yourselves to be true followers of Mine.

(The Message Version)
"Live in me. Make your home in me just as I do in you. In the same way that a branch cannot bear grapes by itself but only by being joined to the vine, you cannot bear fruit unless you are joined with me. "I am the Vine, you are the branches. When you're joined with me and I with you, the relation intimate and organic, the harvest is sure to be abundant. Separated, you cannot produce a thing. Anyone who separates from me is deadwood, gathered up and thrown on the bonfire. But if you make yourselves at home with me and my words are at home in you, you can be sure that whatever you ask will be listened to and acted upon. This is how my Father shows who he is--when you produce grapes, when you mature as my disciples.

Abide in the Greek is *Menōto* and means:

1. to stay (in a given place, state, relation or expectancy)
2. abide, continue, dwell, endure, be present, remain
3. stand, tarry, to sojourn, tarry, not to depart
4. to continue to be present, to be held, kept, continually
5. in reference to time, to continue to be, not to perish, to last, endure
6. of persons, to survive, live, in reference to state or condition
7. to remain as one, not to become another or different

Abiding basically means to live in that state or position; the only way to learn how to abide in the Lord is to spend time resting in His presence. When we abide with the Lord His power, glory, authority, will, character, word, etc., manifests not just in our ministry and lifestyles, but exudes from our very being and sphere of influence. A person who has been abiding with Jesus can captivate an audience and sphere of influence with His authority and boldness that will not only gain ground and Give Him glory, but will manifest miracles, signs and wonders that will transform lives, congregations, atmospheres, communities, generations, nations, and send demons running, especially religious and traditional spirits. I truly believe and have experienced that just like preachers, we can go forth through movement, and souls can be saves, healing and deliverance can manifest, demons can be sent fleeing in torment as shackles are broken eternally, while setting the captives free. Sometimes I meditate on the day that people will get out of wheelchairs and be whole as one goes forth in dance. Such miracles, signs, and wonders only come by spending time soaking and absorbing the power and glory of the Lord, and making His biblical word flesh within you.

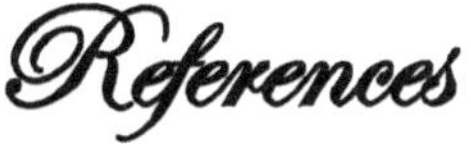

Scripture references are from:

www.blueletterbible.com
www.crosswalk.com

Definitions are quoted from:

www.answers.com
www.m-w.com

KINGDOM SHIFTERS BOOKS & APPAREL

Available at Kingdomshifters.com

BOOKS FOR EVERYONE

Healing The Wounded Leader
The Apostolic Mantle
Kingdom Shifters Decree That Thang
There Is An App For That
Kingdom Watchman Builder On the Wall
Embodiment Of A Kingdom Watchman
Dismantling Homosexuality Handbook
Releasing The Vision
Feasting In His Presence
Kingdom Heirs Decree That Thing
Let There Be Sight
Atmosphere Changers (Weaponry)

BOOKS FOR DANCERS

Dancers! Dancers! Decree That Thang
Spirits That Attack Dance Ministers & Ministries
Dance & Fivefold Ministry

KINGDOM SHIFTER TEE SHIRTS

Kingdom Shifters Tee Shirt

Let The Fruit Speak Tee Shirt
Releasing The Vision Tee Shirt
Kingdom Perspective Tee Shirt
Stand in Position Tee Shirt

No Defense Tee Shirt
My God Rules Like A Boss Tee Shirt
Destiny Blueprint Tee Shirt

KINGDOM SHIFTERS DECREE CD'S

Decree That Thing CD
Kingdom Heirs Decree That Thing CD
Teachings & Worship CD's

www.ingramcontent.com/pod-product-compliance
Lightning Source LLC
LaVergne TN
LVHW010937110826
845149LV00013B/2632

* 9 7 8 0 9 9 9 0 0 4 1 2 8 *